Harvard Business Review

on

REINVENTING YOUR MARKETING

The Harvard Business Review
Paperback series

If you need the best practices and ideas for the business challenges you face—but don't have time to find them—***Harvard Business Review* paperbacks** are for you. Each book is a collection of HBR's inspiring and useful perspectives on a given management topic, all in one place.

The titles include:

Harvard Business Review on Advancing Your Career
Harvard Business Review on Aligning Technology with Strategy
Harvard Business Review on Building Better Teams
Harvard Business Review on Collaborating Effectively
Harvard Business Review on Communicating Effectively
Harvard Business Review on Finding & Keeping the Best People
Harvard Business Review on Fixing Health Care from Inside & Out
Harvard Business Review on Greening Your Business Profitably
Harvard Business Review on Increasing Customer Loyalty
Harvard Business Review on Inspiring & Executing Innovation
Harvard Business Review on Making Smart Decisions
Harvard Business Review on Managing Supply Chains
Harvard Business Review on Rebuilding Your Business Model
Harvard Business Review on Reinventing Your Marketing
Harvard Business Review on Succeeding as an Entrepreneur
Harvard Business Review on Thriving in Emerging Markets
Harvard Business Review on Winning Negotiations

Harvard Business Review

on

REINVENTING YOUR MARKETING

Harvard Business Review Press
Boston, Massachusetts

Copyright 2011 Harvard Business School Publishing Corporation

All rights reserved

Printed in the United States of America

5 4 3 2 1

No part of this publication may be reproduced, stored in or introduced into a retrieval system, or transmitted, in any form, or by any means (electronic, mechanical, photocopying, recording, or otherwise), without the prior permission of the publisher. Requests for permission should be directed to permissions@hbsp.harvard.edu, or mailed to Permissions, Harvard Business School Publishing, 60 Harvard Way, Boston, Massachusetts 02163.

Library of Congress Cataloging-in-Publication Data

Harvard business review on reinventing your marketing.
    p. cm.—(The Harvard business review paperback series)
  Contains articles previously published in the Harvard business review.
  ISBN 978-1-4221-6255-2 (alk. paper)
  1. Marketing. 2. Marketing—Management. 3. Branding (Marketing) 4. Customer relations. I. Harvard business review.
HF5415.H24336 2011
658.8'02—dc22

2011000863

Contents

Rethinking Marketing   1
   Roland T. Rust, Christine Moorman, and Gaurav Bhalla

Unleashing the Power of Marketing   19
   Beth Comstock, Ranjay Gulati, and Stephen Liguori

Marketing Myopia   41
   Theodore Levitt

Marketing Malpractice: The Cause and the Cure   81
   Clayton M. Christensen, Scott Cook, and Taddy Hall

The Brand Report Card   109
   Kevin Lane Keller

The Female Economy   137
   Michael J. Silverstein and Kate Sayre

Customer Value Propositions in Business Markets   155
   James C. Anderson, James A. Narus, and Wouter van Rossum

Getting Brand Communities Right   181
   Susan Fournier and Lara Lee

Aflac's CEO Explains How He Fell for the Duck   203
   Daniel P. Amos

Ending the War Between Sales and Marketing   213
   Philip Kotler, Neil Rackham, and Suj Krishnaswamy

Index   243

Harvard Business Review

on

REINVENTING YOUR MARKETING

Rethinking Marketing

by Roland T. Rust, Christine Moorman, and Gaurav Bhalla

IMAGINE A BRAND MANAGER sitting in his office developing a marketing strategy for his company's new sports drink. He identifies which broad market segments to target, sets prices and promotions, and plans mass media communications. The brand's performance will be measured by aggregate sales and profitability, and his pay and future prospects will hinge on those numbers.

What's wrong with this picture? This firm—like too many—is still managed as if it were stuck in the 1960s, an era of mass markets, mass media, and impersonal transactions. Yet never before have companies had such powerful technologies for interacting directly with customers, collecting and mining information about them, and tailoring their offerings accordingly. And never before have customers expected to interact so deeply with companies, and each other, to shape the products and services they use. To be sure, most companies use customer relationship management and other technologies to get a handle on customers, but no amount of technology can really improve the situation as long as companies are set up to market products rather than cultivate customers. To compete in this aggressively interactive environment, companies must shift their focus from driving transactions to maximizing customer lifetime value. That means making products and brands subservient to long-term customer relationships. And that means changing strategy and structure across the organization—and reinventing the marketing department altogether.

Cultivating Customers

Not long ago, companies looking to get a message out to a large population had only one real option: blanket a huge swath of customers simultaneously, mostly using one-way mass communication. Information about customers consisted primarily of aggregate sales statistics augmented by marketing research data. There was little, if any, direct communication between individual customers and the firm. Today, companies have a host of options at their disposal, making such mass marketing far too crude.

The exhibit "Building relationships" shows where many companies are headed, and all must inevitably go if they hope to remain competitive. The key distinction between a traditional and a customer-cultivating company is that one is organized to push products and brands whereas the other is designed to serve customers

RETHINKING MARKETING

Idea in Brief

Companies have never before had such powerful technologies for understanding and interacting with customers. Yet too many firms operate as if they're stuck in the 1960s, an era of mass marketing, mass media, and impersonal transactions. To compete in an aggressively interactive environment, companies must shift their focus from driving transactions to maximizing customer lifetime value. That means products and brands must be made subservient to customer relationships. And that means transforming the marketing department—traditionally focused on current sales—into a "customer department" by: replacing the CMO with a chief customer officer, cultivating customers rather than pushing products, adopting new performance metrics, and bringing under the marketing umbrella all customer-focused departments, including R&D and customer service.

and customer segments. In the latter, communication is two-way and individualized, or at least tightly targeted at thinly sliced segments. This strategy may be more challenging for firms whose distribution channels own or control customer information—as is the case for many packaged-goods companies. But more and more firms now have access to the rich data they need to make a customer-cultivating strategy work.

B2B companies, for instance, use key account managers and global account directors to focus on meeting customers' evolving needs, rather than selling specific products. IBM organizes according to customer needs, such as energy efficiency or server consolidation, and coordinates its marketing efforts across products for a particular customer. IBM's Insurance Process Acceleration Framework is one example of this service-oriented architecture. Customer and industry specialists in

Building relationships

Product-Manager Driven
Many companies still depend on product managers and one-way mass marketing to push a product to many customers.

Customer-Manager Driven
What's needed is customer managers who engage individual customers or narrow segments in two-way communications, building long-term relationships by promoting whichever of the company's products the customer would value most at any given time.

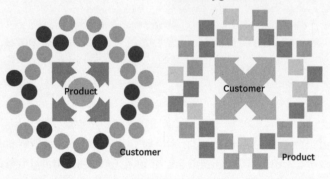

IBM's insurance practice work with lead customers to build fast and flexible processes in areas like claims, new business processing, and underwriting. Instead of focusing on short-term product sales, IBM measures the practice's performance according to long-term customer metrics.

Large B2B firms are often advanced in their customer orientation, and some B2C companies are making notable progress. Increasingly, they view their customer relationships as evolving over time, and they may hand off customers to different parts of the organization selling different brands as their needs change. For instance,

Tesco, a leading UK retailer, has recently made significant investments in analytics that have improved customer retention. Tesco uses its data-collecting loyalty card (the Clubcard) to track which stores customers visit, what they buy, and how they pay. This information has helped Tesco tailor merchandise to local tastes and customize offerings at the individual level across a variety of store formats—from sprawling hypermarts to neighborhood shops. Shoppers who buy diapers for the first time at a Tesco store, for example, receive coupons by mail not only for baby wipes and toys but also for beer, according to a *Wall Street Journal* report. Data analysis revealed that new fathers tend to buy more beer because they can't spend as much time at the pub.

On the services side, American Express actively monitors customers' behavior and responds to changes by offering different products. The firm uses consumer data analysis and algorithms to determine customers' "next best product" according to their changing profiles and to manage risk across cardholders. For example, the first purchase of a upper-class airline ticket on a Gold Card may trigger an invitation to upgrade to a Platinum Card. Or, because of changing circumstances a cardholder may want to give an additional card with a specified spending limit to a child or a contractor. By offering this service, American Express extends existing customers' spending ability to a trusted circle of family members or partners while introducing the brand to potential new customers.

American Express also leverages its strategic position between customers and merchants to create long-term value across both relationships. For instance, the company might use demographic data, customer purchase patterns, and credit information to observe that a cardholder has moved into a new home. AmEx capitalizes on that life event by offering special Membership Rewards on purchases from merchants in its network in the home-furnishings retail category.

One insurance and financial services company we know of also proved adept at tailoring products to customers' life events. Customers who lose a spouse, for example, are flagged for special attention from a team that offers them customized products. When a checking account or credit-card customer gets married, she's a good cross-selling prospect for an auto or home insurance policy and a mortgage. Likewise, the firm targets new empty nesters with home equity loans or investment products and offers renter's insurance to graduating seniors.

Reinventing Marketing

These shining examples aside, boards and C-suites still mostly pay lip service to customer relationships while focusing intently on selling goods and services. Directors and management need to spearhead the strategy shift from transactions to relationships and create the culture, structure, and incentives necessary to execute the strategy.

What does a customer-cultivating organization look like? Although no company has a fully realized customer-focused structure, we can see the features of one in a variety of companies making the transition. The most dramatic change will be the marketing department's reinvention as a "customer department." The first order of business is to replace the traditional CMO with a new type of leader—a chief customer officer.

The CCO

Chief customer officers are increasingly common in companies worldwide—there are more than 300 today, up from 30 in 2003. Companies as diverse as Chrysler, Hershey's, Oracle, Samsung, Sears, United Airlines, Sun Microsystems, and Wachovia now have CCOs. But too often the CCO is merely trying to make a conventional organization more customer-centric. In general, it's a poorly defined role—which may account for CCOs' dubious distinction as having the shortest tenure of all C-suite executives.

To be effective, the CCO role as we conceive it must be a powerful operational position, reporting to the CEO. This executive is responsible for designing and executing the firm's customer relationship strategy and overseeing all customer-facing functions.

A successful CCO promotes a customer-centric culture and removes obstacles to the flow of customer information throughout the organization. This includes getting leaders to regularly engage with customers. At USAA, top managers spend two or three hours a week on the call-center phones with customers. This not only shows employees how serious management is about customer interaction but helps managers understand customers' concerns. Likewise, Tesco managers spend one week a year working in stores and interacting with customers as part of the Tesco Week in Store (TWIST) program.

As managers shift their focus to customers, and customer information increasingly drives decisions, organizational structures that block information flow must be torn down. The reality is that despite large investments in acquiring customer data, most firms underutilize what they know. Information is tightly held, often because of a lack of trust, competition for promotions or resources, and the silo mentality. The CCO must create incentives that eliminate these counterproductive mind-sets.

Ultimately, the CCO is accountable for increasing the profitability of the firm's customers, as measured by metrics such as customer lifetime value (CLV) and customer equity as well as by intermediate indicators, such as word of mouth (or mouse).

Customer Managers

In the new customer department, customer and segment managers identify customers' product needs. Brand managers, under the customer managers' direction, then supply the products that fulfill those needs. This requires shifting resources—principally people and budgets—and authority from product managers to customer managers. (See the sidebar "What Makes a Customer Manager?") This structure is common in the B2B world. In its B2B activities, Procter & Gamble, for instance, has key account managers for major retailers like Wal-Mart. They are less interested in selling, say,

What Makes a Customer Manager?

IN A SENSE, THE ROLE of customer manager is the ultimate expression of marketing (find out what the customer wants and fulfill the need) while the product manager is more aligned with the traditional selling mind-set (have product, find customer).

Jim Spohrer, the director of Global University Programs at IBM, hires what UCal Berkeley professor Morten Hansen calls "T-shaped" people, who have broad expertise with depth in some areas. Customer managers will be most effective when they're T-shaped, combining deep knowledge of particular customers or segments with broad knowledge of the firm and its products. These managers must also be sophisticated data interpreters, able to extract insights from the increasing amount of information about customers' attitudes and activities acquired by mining blogs and other customer forums, monitoring online purchasing behavior, tracking retail sales, and using other types of analytics. While brand managers may be satisfied with examining the media usage statistics associated with their product, brand usage behavior, and brand chat in communities, customer managers will take a broader and more integrative view of the customer. For instance, when P&G managers responsible for the Max Factor and Cover Girl brands spent a week living on the budget of a low-end consumer, they were acting like customer managers. The experience gave these managers important insights into what P&G, not just the specific brands, could do to improve the lives of these customers.

We'd expect the most effective customer managers to have broad training in the social sciences—psychology, anthropology, sociology, and economics—in addition to an understanding of marketing. They'd approach the customer as behavioral scientists rather than as marketing specialists, observing and collecting information about them, interacting with and learning from them, and synthesizing and disseminating what they learned. For business schools to stay relevant in training customer managers, the curriculum needs to shift its emphasis from marketing products to cultivating customers.

Swiffers than in maximizing the value of the customer relationship over the long term. Some B2C companies use this structure as well, foremost among them retail financial institutions that put managers in charge of segments—wealthy customers, college kids, retirees, and so forth—rather than products.

In a customer-cultivating company, a consumer-goods segment manager might offer customers incentives to switch from less-profitable Brand A to more-profitable Brand B. This wouldn't happen in the conventional system, where brand and product managers call the shots. Brand A's manager isn't going to encourage customers to defect—even if that would benefit the company—because he's rewarded for brand performance, not for improving CLV or some other long-term customer metric. This is no small change: It means that product managers must stop focusing on maximizing their products' or brands' profits and become responsible for helping customer and segment managers maximize theirs.

Customer-Facing Functions

As the nexus of customer-facing activity, the customer department assumes responsibility for some of the customer-focused functions that have left the marketing department in recent years and some that have not traditionally been part of it.

CRM. Customer relationship management has been increasingly taken on by companies' IT groups because of the technical capability CRM systems require, according to a Harte-Hanks survey of 300 companies in

Reimagining the marketing department

The traditional marketing department must be reconfigured as a customer department that puts building customer relationships ahead of pushing specific products.

To this end, product managers and customer-focused departments report to a chief customer officer instead of a CMO, and support the strategies of customer or segment managers.

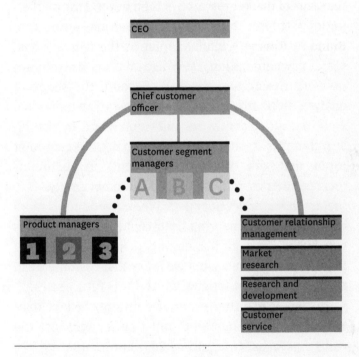

North America: 42% of companies report that CRM is managed by the IT group, 31% by sales, and only 9% by marketing. Yet CRM is, ultimately, a tool for gauging customer needs and behaviors—the new customer department's central role. It makes little sense for the very data required to execute a customer-cultivation strategy to be collected and analyzed outside the customer department. Of course, bringing CRM into the customer department means bringing IT and analytic skills in as well.

Market research. The emphasis of market research changes in a customer-centric company. First, the internal users of market research extend beyond the marketing department to all areas of the organization that touch customers—including finance (the source of customer payment options) and distribution (the source of delivery timing and service). Second, the scope of analysis shifts from an aggregate view to an individual view of customer activities and value. Third, market research shifts its attention to acquiring the customer input that will drive improvements in customer-focused metrics such as CLV and customer equity.

Research and development. When a product is more about clever engineering than customer needs, sales can suffer. For example, engineers like to pack lots of features into products, but we know that customers can suffer from feature fatigue, which hurts future sales.

To make sure that product decisions reflect real-world needs, the customer must be brought into the design process. Integrating R&D and marketing is a good way to do that. Few companies have done this better than Nokia in Asia, where its market share exceeds 60%. In an industry where manufacturers must introduce scores of new offerings every year, the group's ability to translate customer input about features and value into hit product offerings is legendary.

Among its customer-focused innovation tools is Nokia Beta Labs, a virtual developer community that brings users and developer teams together to virtually prototype new features and products, inviting even "wacky ideas" that may never make it to the marketplace. (Nokia adopted a different strategy in the United States, using far less customer input, and has seen its market share slide.)

Examples abound of companies that create new value through the collaboration of users and producers: Mozilla's Firefox in the web browser category, P&G's Swiffer in the home cleaning category, and International Flavors and Fragrances' partnership with B2B customers like Estée Lauder in the perfume market. In a world in which the old R&D-driven models for new product development are giving way to creative collaborations like these, R&D must report to the CCO.

Customer Service
This function should be handled in-house, under the customer department's wing—not only to ensure that the quality of service is high but also to help cultivate long-term relationships. Delta Airlines, for example, recently pulled out of its call centers overseas because cultural differences damaged the airline's ability to interact with North American customers. Delta concluded that the negative impact on the quality of customer relationships wasn't worth the cost savings. Now, when customer service gets a call, a representative immediately identifies the caller's segment and routes her to a customer-service specialist trained to work

with that segment. The interaction is captured in the customer information system and used, in turn, by the customer department to divine new customers' needs and create solutions.

If customer service must be outsourced, the function should report in to a high-level internal customer manager, and its IT infrastructure and customer data must be seamlessly integrated with the company's customer databases.

A New Focus on Customer Metrics

Once companies make the shift from marketing products to cultivating customers, they will need new metrics to gauge the strategy's effectiveness. First, companies need to focus less on product profitability and more on customer profitability. Retailers have applied this concept for some time in their use of loss leaders—products that may be unprofitable but strengthen customer relationships.

Second, companies need to pay less attention to current sales and more to CLV. A company in decline may have good current sales but poor prospects. The customer lifetime value metric evaluates the future profits generated from a customer, properly discounted to reflect the time value of money. Lifetime value focuses the company on long-term health—an emphasis that most shareholders and investors should share. Although too often the markets reward short-term earnings at the expense of future performance, that

New metrics for a new model

The shift from marketing products to cultivating customers demands a shift in metrics as well.

Old approach	New approach
Product profitability	Customer profitability
Current sales	Customer lifetime value
Brand equity	Customer equity
Market share	Customer equity share

unfortunate tendency will change as future-oriented customer metrics become a routine part of financial reporting. An international movement is under way to require companies to report intangible assets in financial statements. As leading indicators such as customer-centered metrics increasingly appear on financial statements, stock prices will begin to reflect them. Even now, savvy analysts are pushing firms to understand customer retention rates and the value of customer and brand assets.

Third, companies need to shift their focus from brand equity (the value of a brand) to customer equity (the sum of the lifetime values of their customers).

Increasing brand equity is best seen as a means to an end, one way to build customer equity (see "Customer-Centered Brand Management," HBR September 2004). Customer equity has the added benefit of being a good proxy for the value of the firm, thereby making marketing more relevant to shareholder value.

Fourth, companies need to pay less attention to current market share and more attention to customer equity share (the value of a company's customer base divided by the total value of the customers in the market). Market share offers a snapshot of the company's competitive sales position at the moment, but customer equity share is a measure of the firm's long-term competitiveness with respect to profitability.

Given the increasing importance of customer-level information, companies must become adept at tracking information at several levels—individual, segment, and aggregate. Different strategic decisions require different levels of information, so companies typically need multiple information sources to meet their needs.

At the individual customer level the key metric is customer lifetime value; the marketing activities tracked most closely are direct marketing activities; and the key sources of data are customer databases that the firm compiles. At the segment level the key metric is the lifetime value of the segment (the lifetime value of the average customer times the number of customers in the segment); the marketing activities tracked most closely are marketing efforts targeted at specific customer segments, sometimes using niche media; and the key sources of information are customer panels and survey data. At the aggregate market level, the key metric is customer equity; the marketing activities tracked most closely are mass marketing efforts, often through mass media; and the key sources of information are aggregate sales data and survey data. We see that firms will typically have a portfolio of information sources.

Clearly, companies need metrics for evaluating progress in collecting and using customer information. How frequently managers contribute to and access customer information archives is a good general measure, although it doesn't reveal much about the quality of the information. To get at that, some firms create markets for new customer information in which employees rate the value of contributions.

Like any other organizational transformation, making a product-focused company fully customer-centric will be difficult. The IT group will want to hang on to CRM; R&D is going to fight hard to keep its relative autonomy; and most important, traditional marketing executives will battle for their jobs. Because the change requires overcoming entrenched interests, it won't happen organically. Transformation must be driven from the top down. But however daunting, the shift is inevitable. It will soon be the only competitive way to serve customers.

ROLAND T. RUST is the David Bruce Smith Chair in Marketing at the University of Maryland's Robert H. Smith School of Business. **CHRISTINE MOORMAN** is the T. Austin

Finch, Sr., Professor of Business Administration at Duke University's Fuqua School of Business. **GAURAV BHALLA** is the president of Knowledge Kinetics, based in Reston, Virginia.

Originally published in January 2010. Reprint R1001F

Unleashing the Power of Marketing

by Beth Comstock, Ranjay Gulati, and Stephen Liguori

JUST 10 YEARS AGO General Electric had no substantial marketing organization. For decades the company had been so confident in its technologies that it seemed to believe the products could market themselves. People designated as marketers were assigned to sales support (lead generation and trade shows, for example) or communications (advertising and promotional materials). In discussions about corporate strategy, marketing wasn't at the table. At best it was considered a support function; at worst, overhead. In a few GE businesses, such as appliances and the former plastics unit, marketing was a viable contributor; but in most of the others, its brilliant minds were languishing in dead-end jobs.

Many internal skeptics did not see how marketing as a function could help GE grow its businesses. Take GE Aviation, the multibillion-dollar division that develops and manufactures jet engines for commercial and military aircraft. The commercial aviation industry is relatively simple: a handful of aircraft manufacturers, two GE competitors (Rolls-Royce and Pratt & Whitney), and about 300 airlines. "You could put the entire industry in a conference room—it's that compact," says Thomas Gentile, the vice president of engine services for GE Aviation and a former chief marketing officer at GE Capital. "So the challenge was how could market research really help us? Because we could literally pick up the phone and call everyone in the industry who mattered and find out what was on their mind."

But things were changing. The businesses were maturing, and like other companies, GE was learning that it could not win simply by launching increasingly sophisticated technologies or by taking existing technologies to new markets. Some of its best-thought-out new offerings were fast becoming commodities. Even executives within a business like Aviation were having trouble making sense of a rapidly changing industry. Fuel prices were volatile; demand was slowing; stronger regulatory oversight was around the corner. How could the business remain competitive and also prosper? "We didn't really know how to translate what we knew about customers into the next growth idea," Gentile admits.

GE's solution was to focus on growth from within, across all businesses—a shift from the past, in which the top line was grown primarily by acquisition and the bottom line by seeking out efficiencies. The refocus ushered in a strategy fueled by technology, innovation, global markets, and stronger customer ties. To succeed,

Idea in Brief

Until a few years ago, General Electric believed that its products could virtually market themselves. Marketers had been limited to passively pushing information to those centrally responsible for innovation—typically in R&D or engineering—with the result that brilliant minds were languishing in dead-end jobs. When it came to discussions about corporate strategy, marketing wasn't at the table. But as GE's businesses matured, the company realized that it could no longer win simply by launching increasingly sophisticated technologies or taking existing technologies to new markets. To succeed, GE would need a marketing engine that could collaborate directly with customers and lead to new markets—one rooted in standards as rigorous as those for functions such as finance and human resources. CEO Jeff Immelt issued a mandate that marketing should be a vital operating function across GE and an engine for organic growth. The marketing team took on the challenge of identifying and codifying from scratch the skills it would need. The result was a marketing framework for the entire company along three dimensions: principles (creating a common language and standards), people (getting the right leaders in place), and process (including very specific measures for grading performance). Marketers took their place alongside technologists and had a voice earlier in the process, as GE's innovation expanded to include ideas grounded in customer needs and market trends.

GE would need a marketing engine that drove more-direct collaboration with customers and led to new markets—one with standards as rigorous as those for functions such as finance and human resources. CEO Jeff Immelt issued a mandate that marketing should be a vital operating function across GE that spurred organic growth.

Recognizing that marketing was vital to all GE units was one thing; acting on that recognition was an entirely different matter. The marketing team took on the challenge of identifying and clearly codifying the modern-day skills it needed. We had to define what success would look like and describe how we would measure results. At the time, GE had no ready or consistent way of calibrating marketing efforts across units, markets, or business models, and we couldn't find one in any textbook. Perhaps most challenging, we had to identify and develop leadership capabilities in our team, whose track record was uneven at best. In the process of creating what we believed would be the definitive marketing function, we arrived at new ways of thinking about marketing skills and about how to compose a first-rate marketing team.

The result was a marketing framework for the entire company along three dimensions: *principles* (creating a common language and standards), *people* (getting the right leaders in place), and *process* (including very specific measures for grading performance). This article focuses on the people aspect, but the three are interdependent and all are critical. Though this is primarily a GE story, its implications are relevant for marketing teams anywhere—and even for people in other functions, because it shows how a team can challenge expectations and perceived limitations.

Not Just a Support Function

Our framework centered on giving marketing a revenue-generating role in its own right. If GE could no longer rely solely on technology breakthroughs for hefty margins, we'd have to find both innovative ways of serving customers based on investments we'd already made and opportunities in new markets, new segments, and new products.

Marketing became the torchbearer for what was internally called "commercial innovation." GE already had a long and rich history as a technology innovator. Now its innovation expanded to include ideas grounded in customer needs and market trends. Marketers took their place alongside technologists and had a voice earlier in the process, to ensure that GE's offerings were differentiated and aimed at the right customer segments. As Immelt saw it, marketing would have a "line" role instead of its historical "staff" role at GE, and would be held responsible for critical operating mechanisms such as pricing and quantifying value for customers. He has pushed GE's global growth with a mantra of "more products at more price points," meaning that GE must not only target high-end users but also apply "just what's needed" technology to better meet customer needs. (See "How GE Is Disrupting Itself," HBR October 2009.)

The proof of marketing's expanded role lay in a series of new cross-company initiatives—among them Imagination Breakthroughs, a portfolio of growth projects created in 2004 and designed to engage marketing and technology in ways that would create new value. These projects get attention, funding, and time to develop, which has been especially important in an economic slowdown, when future-oriented projects are often an easy target for cuts. GE's development of sodium batteries, which was born of the need for new technology to power hybrid locomotives and grew into a stand-alone business that serves telecom and other industries new to GE, was an Imagination Breakthrough. A GE Healthcare offering that combined existing technologies for a new purpose—namely, allowing emergency responders to better distinguish between ischemic and hemorrhagic strokes and then direct patients to the right hospital for care—was another. The Imagination Breakthroughs collectively generate $2 billion in new revenue annually.

Ecomagination, GE's clean-technology initiative, was launched in 2005. It directs investment in R&D and product development in the green and sustainability arena. Now a multitiered business plan, a point of view for the brand, and a purpose for GE's people, Ecomagination has delivered more than 90 new products and $70 billion in revenue in its first five years. In all these initiatives marketing gets into the game at the start, sizing "white space" opportunities, meshing unmet needs with new technologies, and moving our brand in new directions.

"Marketer's DNA"

The marketing leadership at GE had set an ambitious agenda, but no amount of ambition can make up for a dearth of talent. So the team doubled its ranks, from 2,500 in 2003 to 5,000 today. CMO positions were created for all GE's businesses and at the corporate level. These leaders were both tapped from within GE and hired from a number of consumer- and business-oriented companies. More than half of the internal ones lacked formal marketing training. They had started with the company as engineers, salespeople, or Six Sigma leaders and had been promoted because they were strong performers who spoke the same language and grew up in the same industries as their customers. They learned marketing on the job as best they could, given our limited experience. The outside hires were more classically trained; many had MBAs and most had years of proven success at more-sophisticated marketing organizations. We had templates for the roles and responsibilities of these marketers. We expected that the external people would elevate our capabilities, and the internally grown ones would connect the dots culturally. We set up training programs to make sure that over time, all of them could master our core principles. The marketers were only too happy to align themselves with GE's healthy growth during this period.

When the downturn came, in early 2008, we asked ourselves if marketing could perform in a world of slow to no growth. Did we have the skills necessary to create value in tough times? Furthermore, after five years of investment and development, were we any good at marketing? How could we know we were delivering results?

To answer those questions, we conducted an assessment of the marketing team's skills and an audit of its contributions. (See the sidebar "The Maturity Evaluation.") Despite the team's combined knowledge and capability, its impact and results were inconsistent. Why?

The Key Parts of a Marketing Engine

WHEN WE SET OUT TO build a new marketing engine for GE, we realized that success would require three key factors: principles, people, and process. They give marketers across the organization a common language and framework, innovative leadership, and a means of measuring success.

1: Principles

GE long ago created standard procedures and central reservoirs of expertise for functions like finance and HR, but marketing practices varied by product line, unit, or region. From late 2008 through mid-2009 we convened about 30 of our best marketers to develop new standards for our function. We learned that regardless of industry or region, they were struggling with the same issues yet were virtually unaware of one another's existence. So we assigned teams of like-minded subject-matter experts to define the skills we needed to master. They organized eight disciplines into two groups: go-to-market activities (such as segmentation) and commercial essentials (such as branding and communications). To our knowledge, no other company had pulled these

When we looked specifically at marketing leaders, whose skills had to be a priority if we were to make the function a true source of sustainable competitive advantage, we were all the more perplexed. The problem was that the traditional frameworks we had studied didn't provide enough guidance for identifying those skills. The frameworks do an excellent job of outlining marketing principles but not of translating them into action. It became evident that critical behaviors were (a) omitted from classical marketing training, and (b) often underappreciated by GE's operating leaders, in large part because those behaviors were sometimes at odds with the behaviors of other functions.

disciplines into one framework along with detailed definitions of success. We set out to make sure that at least one business could be considered an expert in each category.

2: People

We found that successful marketers play four roles, some of them unusual in marketing: *Instigators* challenge the status quo and look for new and better ways of doing things. *Innovators* turn marketplace insights into untested products, services, or solutions. *Integrators* build bridges across silos and functions and between the company and the market. *Implementers* execute on ideas.

3: Process

Once we knew what we wanted from marketing, we developed metrics for evaluating our teams on the skills defined by our principles. How would we know we were making progress and delivering results? That question led us to a process we call the Maturity Evaluation (see the sidebar later in the article).

We would have to identify the requisite skills ourselves, by studying the people on the team who were excelling. We learned that four fundamental roles are needed to transform marketing into a strategic function: instigator, innovator, integrator, and implementer. We call them "marketer's DNA." Each role has become absolutely crucial at GE.

The Instigator

Marketing leaders need to think strategically and challenge the status quo, using their unique external vantage point to see what may not be apparent to others

The Maturity Evaluation

How We Measure Ourselves

In the spring of 2010 every CMO at General Electric convened all his or her marketing teams (each has about 10) for what will become an annual self-evaluation. It measures performance in eight major capability areas, each requiring specific skills with detailed definitions. For each capability we offer a description of what success looks like and how we measure it. The level of granularity and precision—we have a total of 35 skills and 140 definitions—makes it impossible to fake your way through.

The teams score their units' 35 skills from 1 (minimal) to 4 (recognized by industry peers as best in class) and review their assessments with business leaders to make sure they're realistic and relevant to unit goals. We then roll up the scores to the eight capability areas. When the scores are aligned across the organization, the result is a summary map that clearly shows where we are falling short—and where we have pockets of strength. A business might discover, for instance, that its marketers are good at pricing but the weakest in the company on branding and communications. The value of a common language, rigor, and process across a previously highly subjective function cannot be overstated. Aviation, for instance, can compare notes with Healthcare. This is proving to be very engaging within and across business units.

---

in the business. Sometimes this entails moving beyond preaching about marketing's merits to imagining scenarios that business heads might face—perhaps marketing's most important role. Leaders must be willing to push change. But the hard truth is that any affection for change agents dissolves when people don't like what's being proposed. Perhaps that explains why, according to

We now have hundreds of completed self-audits, giving CMOs and CEOs a benchmark against which to measure improvement.

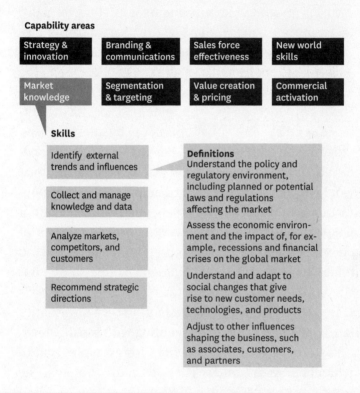

several surveys, CMOs last only 23 months, on average—just over half the tenure of other C-level positions.

According to Jean-Michel Cossery, the vice president and CMO of GE Healthcare, his division had traditionally acted as a "technology pusher." "We had a tendency to develop products because we could do it and not because they were wanted in the market," he says. That approach was unsustainable. After Congress enacted the Deficit Reduction Act of 2005, wiping $13 billion out of medical-imaging reimbursements virtually overnight, GE Healthcare had to explore new markets and offerings.

Cossery started an internal incubator fund that enlisted and sponsored a small skunkworks to scan the entire business landscape, as opposed to thinking only about a product or a P&L silo, and come up with marketing ideas that were either not on the business leaders' radar or considered elusive. For example, Cossery believed that the health care system existing in 2005 would not be able to meet the demands of an aging population that wanted to be independent and stay out of hospitals. In combination with a growing number of chronic-care patients, this represented a potential $10 billion market with huge commercial opportunity. But GE didn't have an offering for that market. Cossery's team connected with scientists from GE's informatics lab, which had been experimenting with sensing technology to track human activity—for example, that of patients in their homes. They created a "home of the future" at GE's R&D center in Niskayuna, New York. The team built algorithms tied to patients' movements and even conducted tests in the homes of researchers' elderly parents.

Cossery's team ran into internal resistance because some viewed the project as too small for GE's target of hospitals and large physician practices. But ultimately, armed with research findings and product prototypes, marketing joined with product development to launch the QuietCare home sensing system. Home health is now a stand-alone business and a priority for GE Healthcare. It's still nascent, and enthusiasm for it isn't unanimous, but hospital clients have begun asking for home solutions to prevent readmittance. This past August, GE announced a joint venture with Intel to speed the progress of home health-monitoring innovations.

The Innovator

While it was relegated to a support function at much of GE, marketing had been limited to passing information along to those centrally responsible for innovation—typically R&D or engineering. The marketers might, for instance, recognize a customer trend and communicate it to the product R&D department. Or they might be called on to develop a creative advertising campaign for a new product. Other than that, marketing groups and CMOs had no consistently good grasp of how to shape the company's innovation agenda. We had to expand our thinking beyond product features and functionality to include pricing, delivery, customer engagement, complicated risk-reward sharing, and new business models—all part of commercial innovation.

This was familiar territory for Lorraine Bolsinger, the president of systems of GE Aviation, who was its CMO when she led the business into the very light jet space—think "air taxis" that carry four to six passengers to small regional airports—in 2004. The idea of air taxis seemed crazy to most people at GE Aviation. Why did the business need to be in that market when it was doing well in the large commercial and military space?

Keep in mind that engine development cycles can last a decade or more. Commitment to a new space is a big commitment to the future.

Bolsinger and her team nonetheless believed that this market was important to GE. The commercial airline industry had been steadily moving away from a hub-and-spoke system to a point-to-point system, led by the boom in regional jets. Why not go even smaller? It was tough to get people to listen at first, but Bolsinger brought in entrepreneurial air taxi operators who were smart and sophisticated and could explain how their business model differed from the traditional jet model. GE's engine-design expertise, greater than its competitors', could add significant value by lowering operating costs (through burning less fuel) and increasing asset utilization (through better reliability and longer cycles), making the economics work for air taxi operators.

More recently the Aviation marketers realized that their business was selling engines on the basis of thrust and other quantitative metrics, whereas it could be selling on the basis of operational efficiency and resource productivity. That research-fed insight led, for example, to myEngines, which provides customers with real-time service updates for their aircraft engines: what repairs are required, how long they will take, how much they will cost, and so on. The information can be conveniently delivered to customers' smartphones or tablets.

The inspiration for myEngines came from Tim Swords, a marketing executive at GE Aviation, who thought of it as a Facebook for engines. He and his team introduced a pilot program to test applications with a small group of customers. The response was overwhelmingly positive, strengthening a business case that led to funding for full development. The application was commercially launched at the 2010 Farnborough International Airshow, with an announcement that its first customer, LAN Airlines of Chile, had selected myEngines for its entire fleet of some 100 aircraft.

Innovative marketers use unique marketplace insights to come up with products, services, or solutions based on untested ideas. P&G and other consumer-facing companies take that broad view of innovation, but it has been slow to develop at traditionally business-focused companies like GE. The more an idea deviates from the status quo, the greater the market opportunity—and, of course, the larger the personal risk to whoever is pushing the idea. Marketing leaders need not only the courage to pursue bold initiatives but also the persistence and political skills to overcome naysayers. Before the business model and payback for myEngines were clear, Thomas Gentile recalls, "we had to fight tooth and nail to get the resources we needed."

The Integrator

An integrator builds bridges across multiple organizational silos and functions to unite them on a single path. Sometimes he or she must act as a "translator," making outside customer insights relevant and meaningful to those inside the organization. Marketing is uniquely positioned to do this, but when we began, the team was nowhere near being capable of that role. We realized that we would have to speak product language to R&D and customer language to the sales force—to unite customer-facing functions with the back of the organization and enable the company to cross-sell bundled products.

In other cases integration may simply mean bringing disparate groups in the organization together to collectively assess market dynamics. Consider GE Capital. Perhaps no other GE business has gone through as much upheaval in the past two years. Previously, GE Capital had been mostly a deal shop. "We had abundant liquidity and would try to find every deal that was out there," recalls Lee Cooper, the vice president and CMO of GE Capital, Americas. But the global recession racked the industry in 2008. "We were looking at our business shrinking from about $650 billion in assets down to about $450 billion," Cooper says.

So Cooper and Dan Henson, the CEO of GE Capital, Americas (and a former corporate CMO), set up a weekly "war room" in which the division's senior leaders would look at key metrics—margins, pricing, customer pipelines, and so on—of its different businesses and take quick action to address any issues that surfaced. Before the crisis, the division had reviewed many portfolios in aggregate, checking on business and industry health indicators monthly or even quarterly. Speeding up the process allowed GE Capital to quickly reallocate resources when necessary. For instance, as losses mounted, it terminated sales efforts in certain industry sectors and redeployed the sales teams to healthier ones, netting billions of dollars' worth of new assets.

More than 20 GE Capital executives participate weekly in the war room, including the heads of the business units, the CEO, the CMO, the CFO, the CIO, the general counsel, the head of operations, chief risk officers, the head of business development, and the head of HR. Things get done—they don't get stuck in committees or mired in analysis paralysis. In fact, the war room concept has been so successful that the individual business units now have their own miniversions.

"At first the war room was a process, but it's since become more of a mentality for making commercial decisions and for instilling accountability," Cooper explains. "It's become part of our culture." Indeed, GE Capital plans to continue the practice even after the economy rebounds. "The danger is that when we get out of this recession, we don't manage our business with the discipline and rigor that is needed," he says. "But that would just put us in the position of not being able to respond to the next recession until it's too late."

The Implementer

All leaders must be able to execute, but marketing executives have to be particularly skillful in this area because they often don't have much organizational clout. At GE, if you don't run a P&L business, it's assumed that you probably don't have the influence to drive change. So marketing leaders have to build coalitions and persuade others, using functional expertise, insights, and teamwork rather than authority. They have to mobilize people and, quite simply, get things done. Marketers are too often painted as ideas people who don't stick around to see their ideas implemented or as wonks who prescribe heavy doses of theory. So if they want credibility, they have to deliver results.

Marketing leaders at GE Energy, the multibillion-dollar division that sells generators, gas and wind turbines, transformers, and other energy-related products and services, realized that its different P&L groups had no common methodology for assessing competitors from a big-picture perspective. "Everyone was taking a parochial view, from a particular business unit or product standpoint," recalls Mark Dudzinski, the CMO at GE Energy. They relied on internal perspectives and anecdotal input; competitive intelligence consisted largely of passing along articles containing information about rivals.

So marketing spearheaded the establishment of a Center of Excellence (COE) that would gather and disseminate key competitor information. The intent was to offer insightful analysis as well as original research. The center started by publishing a quarterly overview of each major competitor that included basics such as the competitor's versus GE's financial results, what analysts were saying, what the competitor's executives were saying, and the competitor's big wins. But the COE's biggest contribution is its delineation of potential scenarios, which anticipate, for example, price moves, growth into new markets, product innovation, and acquisitions.

The COE did indeed analyze and predict as well as report. In one case it foresaw which companies would enter a certain segment of the power generation market and which wouldn't, which helped GE craft its own strategy for that business. (For example, one analysis indicated that GE should not respond to a competitor's low bids because its prices appeared unsustainable given its business model, which would not change because it was the competitor's cash cow.) It also foresaw which companies would build new, larger gas turbines and which would not, affecting GE's investment in new products. In another case the COE teamed with HR to analyze what kinds of talent competitors were hiring globally and then predict what products they were most likely developing. "We went from offering tactical advice—how to compete against a particular company, for instance—to providing more strategic industry information," Dudzinski says.

As word of its early successes spread, the Center of Excellence was asked to consult on various projects. Its data and insights are now part of GE Energy's weekly operational meetings, making marketing an integral component of the business's decision making process.

A Path Forward

We've discussed the four components of marketer's DNA as separate behaviors and actions, but any ambitious marketing effort requires that they be in concert. All four are essential, but a marketing leader who has them all is rare. Fortunately, the function doesn't require such a person. One GE business has two CMOs with complementary areas of expertise: The first is exceptionally good at integrating with other functions, especially technology and sales, and at getting things done. The second peers around corners to decipher and analyze key trends and industry expectations.

That said, GE is quick to recognize and reward marketing leaders with the right DNA. We identify our top 50 up-and-coming marketers as "rock stars" and make their development a company priority. They receive additional coaching and career counseling, and GE includes them in planning the marketing function's future.

For the first time, GE is treating marketing as a critical function—one for all seasons. This energizes our marketing community and prompts constructive dialogue with executive teams. We're building an extensive system to circulate best practices and embed them in every business unit. We started an internal social network called MarkNet—a real silo buster. More than two-thirds of our global team members now blog and communicate across businesses, levels, and geographies. Our quarterly Marketing Council sets the stage for cross-business and intrabusiness projects and gives GE marketers around the world an easily understood language and framework.

GE's marketing transformation is a work in progress. We continue to test new value propositions, to develop new customer-oriented metrics, and to explore opportunities for making digital connections with the marketplace. We have gained momentum through significant wins, but we have yet to achieve our true goal: "gold standard" marketing throughout the organization. The journey continues.

BETH COMSTOCK is the chief marketing officer and a senior vice president of General Electric. **RANJAY GULATI** is the Jaime and Josefina Chua Tiampo Professor at Harvard Business School and the author of *Reorganize for Resilience* (Harvard Business Review Press, 2010). **STEPHEN LIGUORI** is the executive director of global marketing at General Electric.

Originally published in October 2010. Reprint R1010H

Marketing Myopia

by Theodore Levitt

EVERY MAJOR INDUSTRY was once a growth industry. But some that are now riding a wave of growth enthusiasm are very much in the shadow of decline. Others that are thought of as seasoned growth industries have actually stopped growing. In every case, the reason growth is threatened, slowed, or stopped is *not* because the market is saturated. It is because there has been a failure of management.

Fateful Purposes

The failure is at the top. The executives responsible for it, in the last analysis, are those who deal with broad aims and policies. Thus:

- The railroads did not stop growing because the need for passenger and freight transportation declined. That grew. The railroads are in trouble today not because that need was filled by others (cars, trucks, airplanes, and even telephones) but because it was *not* filled by the railroads themselves. They let others take customers away from them because they assumed themselves to be in the railroad business rather than in the transportation business. The reason they defined their industry incorrectly was that they were railroad oriented instead of transportation oriented; they were product oriented instead of customer oriented.

- Hollywood barely escaped being totally ravished by television. Actually, all the established film companies went through drastic reorganizations. Some simply disappeared. All of them got into trouble not because of TV's inroads but because of their own myopia. As with the railroads, Hollywood defined its business incorrectly. It thought it was in the movie business when it was actually in the entertainment business. "Movies" implied a specific, limited product. This produced a fatuous contentment that from the beginning led producers to view TV as a threat. Hollywood scorned and rejected TV when it should have welcomed it as an opportunity—an opportunity to expand the entertainment business.

Today, TV is a bigger business than the old narrowly defined movie business ever was. Had Hollywood been customer oriented (providing entertainment) rather than product oriented (making movies), would it have gone through the fiscal purgatory that it did? I doubt it. What ultimately saved Hollywood and accounted for its resurgence was the wave of new young writers, producers, and directors whose previous successes in

Idea in Brief

What business are you *really* in? A seemingly obvious question—but one we should all ask *before* demand for our companies' products or services dwindles.

The railroads failed to ask this same question—and stopped growing. Why? Not because people no longer needed transportation. And not because other innovations (cars, airplanes) filled transportation needs. Rather, railroads stopped growing because *railroads* didn't move to fill those needs. Their executives incorrectly thought that they were in the railroad business, not the transportation business. They viewed themselves as providing a product instead of serving customers. Too many other industries make the same mistake—putting themselves at risk of obsolescence.

How to ensure continued growth for your company? Concentrate on meeting customers' needs rather than selling products. Chemical powerhouse DuPont kept a close eye on its customers' most pressing concerns—and deployed its technical know-how to create an ever-expanding array of products that appealed to customers and continuously enlarged its market. If DuPont had merely found more uses for its flagship invention, nylon, it might not be around today.

---

television had decimated the old movie companies and toppled the big movie moguls.

There are other, less obvious examples of industries that have been and are now endangering their futures by improperly defining their purposes. I shall discuss some of them in detail later and analyze the kind of policies that lead to trouble. Right now, it may help to show what a thoroughly customer-oriented management can do to keep a growth industry growing, even after the obvious opportunities have been exhausted, and here there are two examples that have been around for a long time. They are nylon and glass—specifically,

Idea in Practice

We put our businesses at risk of obsolescence when we accept any of the following myths:

Myth 1: An ever-expanding and more affluent population will ensure our growth. When markets are expanding, we often assume we don't have to think imaginatively about our businesses. Instead, we seek to outdo rivals simply by improving on what we're already doing. The consequence: We increase the efficiency of *making* our products, rather than boosting the value those products deliver to customers.

Myth 2: There is no competitive substitute for our industry's major product. Believing that our products have no rivals makes our companies vulnerable to dramatic innovations from outside our industries—often by smaller, newer companies that are focusing on customer needs rather than the products themselves.

Myth 3: We can protect ourselves through mass production. Few of us can resist the prospect of the increased profits that come with steeply declining unit costs. But focusing on mass production emphasizes our *company's* needs—when we should be emphasizing our *customers'*.

Myth 4: Technical research and development will ensure our growth. When R&D produces breakthrough products, we may be tempted to organize our companies around the technology rather than the consumer. Instead, we should remain focused on satisfying customer needs.

E.I. du Pont de Nemours and Company and Corning Glass Works.

Both companies have great technical competence. Their product orientation is unquestioned. But this alone does not explain their success. After all, who was more pridefully product oriented and product conscious than the erstwhile New England textile companies that have been so thoroughly massacred? The DuPonts and the Cornings have succeeded not primarily because of their product or research orientation but because they have been thoroughly customer oriented also. It is constant watchfulness for opportunities to apply their technical know-how to the creation of customer-satisfying uses that accounts for their prodigious output of successful new products. Without a very sophisticated eye on the customer, most of their new products might have been wrong, their sales methods useless.

Aluminum has also continued to be a growth industry, thanks to the efforts of two wartime-created companies that deliberately set about inventing new customer-satisfying uses. Without Kaiser Aluminum & Chemical Corporation and Reynolds Metals Company, the total demand for aluminum today would be vastly less.

Error of Analysis

Some may argue that it is foolish to set the railroads off against aluminum or the movies off against glass. Are not aluminum and glass naturally so versatile that the industries are bound to have more growth opportunities than the railroads and the movies? This view commits precisely the error I have been talking about. It defines an industry or a product or a cluster of know-how so narrowly as to guarantee its premature senescence. When we mention "railroads," we should make sure we mean "transportation." As transporters, the railroads still have a good chance for very considerable growth. They are not limited to the railroad business as such (though in my opinion, rail transportation is potentially a much stronger transportation medium than is generally believed).

What the railroads lack is not opportunity but some of the managerial imaginativeness and audacity that made them great. Even an amateur like Jacques Barzun can see what is lacking when he says, "I grieve to see the most advanced physical and social organization of the last century go down in shabby disgrace for lack of the same comprehensive imagination that built it up. [What is lacking is] the will of the companies to survive and to satisfy the public by inventiveness and skill."[1]

Shadow of Obsolescence

It is impossible to mention a single major industry that did not at one time qualify for the magic appellation of "growth industry." In each case, the industry's assumed strength lay in the apparently unchallenged superiority of its product. There appeared to be no effective substitute for it. It was itself a runaway substitute for the product it so triumphantly replaced. Yet one after another of these celebrated industries has come under a shadow. Let us look briefly at a few more of them, this time taking examples that have so far received a little less attention.

Dry Cleaning

This was once a growth industry with lavish prospects. In an age of wool garments, imagine being finally able to get them clean safely and easily. The boom was on. Yet here we are 30 years after the boom started, and the industry is in trouble. Where has the competition come from? From a better way of cleaning? No. It has come from synthetic fibers and chemical additives that have cut the need for dry cleaning. But this is only the beginning. Lurking in the wings and ready to make chemical dry cleaning totally obsolete is that powerful magician, ultrasonics.

Electric Utilities

This is another one of those supposedly "no substitute" products that has been enthroned on a pedestal of invincible growth. When the incandescent lamp came along, kerosene lights were finished. Later, the waterwheel and the steam engine were cut to ribbons by the flexibility, reliability, simplicity, and just plain easy availability of electric motors. The prosperity of electric utilities continues to wax extravagant as the home is converted into a museum of electric gadgetry. How can anybody miss by investing in utilities, with no competition, nothing but growth ahead?

But a second look is not quite so comforting. A score of nonutility companies are well advanced toward developing a powerful chemical fuel cell, which could sit in some hidden closet of every home silently ticking off electric power. The electric lines that vulgarize so many neighborhoods would be eliminated. So would the endless demolition of streets and service interruptions during storms. Also on the horizon is solar energy, again pioneered by nonutility companies.

Who says that the utilities have no competition? They may be natural monopolies now, but tomorrow they may be natural deaths. To avoid this prospect, they too will have to develop fuel cells, solar energy, and other power sources. To survive, they themselves will have to plot the obsolescence of what now produces their livelihood.

Grocery Stores
Many people find it hard to realize that there ever was a thriving establishment known as the "corner store." The supermarket took over with a powerful effectiveness. Yet the big food chains of the 1930s narrowly escaped being completely wiped out by the aggressive expansion of independent supermarkets. The first genuine supermarket was opened in 1930, in Jamaica, Long Island. By 1933, supermarkets were thriving in California, Ohio, Pennsylvania, and elsewhere. Yet the established chains pompously ignored them. When they chose to notice them, it was with such derisive descriptions as "cheapy," "horse-and-buggy," "cracker-barrel storekeeping," and "unethical opportunists."

The executive of one big chain announced at the time that he found it "hard to believe that people will drive for miles to shop for foods and sacrifice the personal service chains have perfected and to which [the consumer] is accustomed."[2] As late as 1936, the National Wholesale Grocers convention and the New Jersey Retail Grocers Association said there was nothing to fear. They said that the supers' narrow appeal to the price buyer limited the size of their market. They had to draw from miles around. When imitators came, there would be wholesale liquidations as volume fell. The high sales of the supers were said to be partly due to their novelty.

People wanted convenient neighborhood grocers. If the neighborhood stores would "cooperate with their suppliers, pay attention to their costs, and improve their service," they would be able to weather the competition until it blew over.[3]

It never blew over. The chains discovered that survival required going into the supermarket business. This meant the wholesale destruction of their huge investments in corner store sites and in established distribution and merchandising methods. The companies with "the courage of their convictions" resolutely stuck to the corner store philosophy. They kept their pride but lost their shirts.

A Self-Deceiving Cycle

But memories are short. For example, it is hard for people who today confidently hail the twin messiahs of electronics and chemicals to see how things could possibly go wrong with these galloping industries. They probably also cannot see how a reasonably sensible businessperson could have been as myopic as the famous Boston millionaire who early in the twentieth century unintentionally sentenced his heirs to poverty by stipulating that his entire estate be forever invested exclusively in electric streetcar securities. His posthumous declaration, "There will always be a big demand for efficient urban transportation," is no consolation to his heirs, who sustain life by pumping gasoline at automobile filling stations.

Yet, in a casual survey I took among a group of intelligent business executives, nearly half agreed that it would be hard to hurt their heirs by tying their estates forever to the electronics industry. When I then confronted them with the Boston streetcar example, they chorused unanimously, "That's different!" But is it? Is not the basic situation identical?

In truth, *there is no such thing as a growth industry,* I believe. There are only companies organized and operated to create and capitalize on growth opportunities. Industries that assume themselves to be riding some automatic growth escalator invariably descend into stagnation. The history of every dead and dying "growth" industry shows a self-deceiving cycle of bountiful expansion and undetected decay. There are four conditions that usually guarantee this cycle:

1. The belief that growth is assured by an expanding and more affluent population;

2. The belief that there is no competitive substitute for the industry's major product;

3. Too much faith in mass production and in the advantages of rapidly declining unit costs as output rises;

4. Preoccupation with a product that lends itself to carefully controlled scientific experimentation, improvement, and manufacturing cost reduction.

I should like now to examine each of these conditions in some detail. To build my case as boldly as possible, I shall illustrate the points with reference to three industries: petroleum, automobiles, and electronics. I'll focus on petroleum in particular, because it spans more years and more vicissitudes. Not only do these three industries have excellent reputations with the general public and also enjoy the confidence of sophisticated investors, but their managements have become known for progressive thinking in areas like financial control, product research, and management training. If obsolescence can cripple even these industries, it can happen anywhere.

Population Myth

The belief that profits are assured by an expanding and more affluent population is dear to the heart of every industry. It takes the edge off the apprehensions everybody understandably feels about the future. If consumers are multiplying and also buying more of your product or service, you can face the future with considerably more comfort than if the market were shrinking. An expanding market keeps the manufacturer from having to think very hard or imaginatively. If thinking is an intellectual response to a problem, then the absence of a problem leads to the absence of thinking. If your product has an automatically expanding market, then you will not give much thought to how to expand it.

One of the most interesting examples of this is provided by the petroleum industry. Probably our oldest growth industry, it has an enviable record. While there are some current concerns about its growth rate, the industry itself tends to be optimistic.

But I believe it can be demonstrated that it is undergoing a fundamental yet typical change. It is not only ceasing to be a growth industry but may actually be a declining one, relative to other businesses. Although there is widespread unawareness of this fact, it is conceivable that in time, the oil industry may find itself in much the same position of retrospective glory that the railroads are now in. Despite its pioneering work in developing and applying the present-value method of investment evaluation, in employee relations, and in working with developing countries, the petroleum business is a distressing example of how complacency and wrongheadedness can stubbornly convert opportunity into near disaster.

One of the characteristics of this and other industries that have believed very strongly in the beneficial consequences of an expanding population, while at the same time having a generic product for which there has appeared to be no competitive substitute, is that the individual companies have sought to outdo their competitors by improving on what they are already doing. This makes sense, of course, if one assumes that sales are tied to the country's population strings, because the customer can compare products only on a feature-by-feature basis. I believe it is significant, for example, that not since John D. Rockefeller sent free kerosene lamps to China has the oil industry done anything really outstanding to create a demand for its product. Not even in product improvement has it showered itself with eminence. The greatest single improvement—the development of tetraethyl lead—came from outside the industry, specifically from General Motors and DuPont. The big contributions made by the industry itself are confined to the technology of oil exploration, oil production, and oil refining.

Asking for Trouble

In other words, the petroleum industry's efforts have focused on improving the *efficiency* of getting and making its product, not really on improving the generic product or its marketing. Moreover, its chief product has continually been defined in the narrowest possible terms—namely, gasoline, not energy, fuel, or transportation. This attitude has helped assure that:

- Major improvements in gasoline quality tend not to originate in the oil industry. The development of superior alternative fuels also comes from outside the oil industry, as will be shown later.

- Major innovations in automobile fuel marketing come from small, new oil companies that are not primarily preoccupied with production or refining. These are the companies that have been responsible for the rapidly expanding multipump gasoline stations, with their successful emphasis on large and clean layouts, rapid and efficient driveway service, and quality gasoline at low prices.

Thus, the oil industry is asking for trouble from outsiders. Sooner or later, in this land of hungry investors and entrepreneurs, a threat is sure to come. The possibility of this will become more apparent when we turn to the next dangerous belief of many managements. For the sake of continuity, because this second belief is tied closely to the first, I shall continue with the same example.

The Idea of Indispensability

The petroleum industry is pretty much convinced that there is no competitive substitute for its major product, gasoline—or, if there is, that it will continue to be a derivative of crude oil, such as diesel fuel or kerosene jet fuel.

There is a lot of automatic wishful thinking in this assumption. The trouble is that most refining companies own huge amounts of crude oil reserves. These have value only if there is a market for products into which oil can be converted. Hence the tenacious belief in the continuing competitive superiority of automobile fuels made from crude oil.

This idea persists despite all historic evidence against it. The evidence not only shows that oil has never been a superior product for any purpose for very long but also that the oil industry has never really been a growth industry. Rather, it has been a succession of different businesses that have gone through the usual historic cycles of growth, maturity, and decay. The industry's overall survival is owed to a series of miraculous escapes from total obsolescence, of last-minute and unexpected reprieves from total disaster reminiscent of the perils of Pauline.

The Perils of Petroleum

To illustrate, I shall sketch in only the main episodes. First, crude oil was largely a patent medicine. But even before that fad ran out, demand was greatly expanded by the use of oil in kerosene lamps. The prospect of lighting the world's lamps gave rise to an extravagant promise of growth. The prospects were similar to those the industry now holds for gasoline in other parts of the world. It can hardly wait for the underdeveloped nations to get a car in every garage.

In the days of the kerosene lamp, the oil companies competed with each other and against gaslight by trying to improve the illuminating characteristics of kerosene. Then suddenly the impossible happened. Edison invented a light that was totally nondependent on crude oil. Had it not been for the growing use of kerosene in space heaters, the incandescent lamp would have completely finished oil as a growth industry at that time. Oil would have been good for little else than axle grease.

Then disaster and reprieve struck again. Two great innovations occurred, neither originating in the oil industry. First, the successful development of coal-burning domestic central-heating systems made the space heater obsolete. While the industry reeled, along came its most magnificent boost yet: the internal combustion engine, also invented by outsiders. Then, when the prodigious expansion for gasoline finally began to level off in the 1920s, along came the miraculous escape of the central oil heater. Once again, the escape was provided by an outsider's invention and development. And when that market weakened, wartime demand for aviation fuel came to the rescue. After the war, the expansion of civilian aviation, the dieselization of railroads, and the explosive demand for cars and trucks kept the industry's growth in high gear.

Meanwhile, centralized oil heating—whose boom potential had only recently been proclaimed—ran into severe competition from natural gas. While the oil companies themselves owned the gas that now competed with their oil, the industry did not originate the natural gas revolution, nor has it to this day greatly profited from its gas ownership. The gas revolution was made by newly formed transmission companies that marketed the product with an aggressive ardor. They started a magnificent new industry, first against the advice and then against the resistance of the oil companies.

By all the logic of the situation, the oil companies themselves should have made the gas revolution. They not only owned the gas, they also were the only people experienced in handling, scrubbing, and using it and the only people experienced in pipeline technology and transmission. They also understood heating problems. But, partly because they knew that natural gas would compete with their own sale of heating oil, the oil companies pooh-poohed the potential of gas. The revolution was finally started by oil pipeline executives who, unable to persuade their own companies to go into gas, quit and organized the spectacularly successful gas transmission companies. Even after their success became painfully evident to the oil companies, the latter did not go into gas transmission. The multibillion-dollar business that should have been theirs went to others. As in the past, the industry was blinded by its narrow preoccupation with a specific product and the value of its reserves. It paid little or no attention to its customers' basic needs and preferences.

The postwar years have not witnessed any change. Immediately after World War II, the oil industry was greatly encouraged about its future by the rapid increase in demand for its traditional line of products. In 1950, most companies projected annual rates of domestic expansion of around 6% through at least 1975. Though the ratio of crude oil reserves to demand in the free world was about 20 to 1, with 10 to 1 being usually considered a reasonable working ratio in the United States, booming demand sent oil explorers searching for more without sufficient regard to what the future really promised. In 1952, they "hit" in the Middle East; the ratio skyrocketed to 42 to 1. If gross additions to reserves continue at the average rate of the past five years (37 billion barrels annually), then by 1970, the reserve ratio will be up to 45 to 1. This abundance of oil has weakened crude and product prices all over the world.

An Uncertain Future

Management cannot find much consolation today in the rapidly expanding petrochemical industry, another oil-using idea that did not originate in the leading firms. The total U.S. production of petrochemicals is equivalent to about 2% (by volume) of the demand for all petroleum products. Although the petrochemical industry is now expected to grow by about 10% per year, this will not offset other drains on the growth of crude oil consumption. Furthermore, while petrochemical products are many and growing, it is important to remember that there are nonpetroleum sources of the basic raw material, such as coal. Besides, a lot of plastics can be produced with relatively little oil. A 50,000-barrel-per-day oil refinery is now considered the absolute minimum size for efficiency. But a 5,000-barrel-per-day chemical plant is a giant operation.

Oil has never been a continuously strong growth industry. It has grown by fits and starts, always miraculously saved by innovations and developments not of its own making. The reason it has not grown in a smooth progression is that each time it thought it had a superior product safe from the possibility of competitive substitutes, the product turned out to be inferior and notoriously subject to obsolescence. Until now, gasoline (for motor fuel, anyhow) has escaped this fate. But, as we shall see later, it too may be on its last legs.

The point of all this is that there is no guarantee against product obsolescence. If a company's own research does not make a product obsolete, another's will. Unless an industry is especially lucky, as oil has been until now, it can easily go down in a sea of red figures—just as the railroads have, as the buggy whip manufacturers have, as the corner grocery chains have, as most of the big movie companies have, and, indeed, as many other industries have.

The best way for a firm to be lucky is to make its own luck. That requires knowing what makes a business successful. One of the greatest enemies of this knowledge is mass production.

Production Pressures

Mass production industries are impelled by a great drive to produce all they can. The prospect of steeply declining unit costs as output rises is more than most companies can usually resist. The profit possibilities look spectacular. All effort focuses on production. The result is that marketing gets neglected.

John Kenneth Galbraith contends that just the opposite occurs.[4] Output is so prodigious that all effort concentrates on trying to get rid of it. He says this accounts for singing commercials, the desecration of the countryside with advertising signs, and other wasteful and vulgar practices. Galbraith has a finger on something real, but he misses the strategic point. Mass production does indeed generate great pressure to "move" the product. But what usually gets emphasized is selling, not marketing. Marketing, a more sophisticated and complex process, gets ignored.

The difference between marketing and selling is more than semantic. Selling focuses on the needs of the seller, marketing on the needs of the buyer. Selling is preoccupied with the seller's need to convert the product into cash, marketing with the idea of satisfying the needs of the customer by means of the product and the whole cluster of things associated with creating, delivering, and, finally, consuming it.

In some industries, the enticements of full mass production have been so powerful that top management in effect has told the sales department, "You get rid of it; we'll worry about profits." By contrast, a truly marketing-minded firm tries to create value-satisfying goods and services that consumers will want to buy. What it offers for sale includes not only the generic product or service but also how it is made available to the customer, in what form, when, under what conditions, and at what terms of trade. Most important, what it offers for sale is determined not by the seller but by the buyer. The seller takes cues from the buyer in such a way that the product becomes a consequence of the marketing effort, not vice versa.

A Lag in Detroit

This may sound like an elementary rule of business, but that does not keep it from being violated wholesale. It is certainly more violated than honored. Take the automobile industry.

Here mass production is most famous, most honored, and has the greatest impact on the entire society. The industry has hitched its fortune to the relentless requirements of the annual model change, a policy that makes customer orientation an especially urgent necessity. Consequently, the auto companies annually spend millions of dollars on consumer research. But the fact that the new compact cars are selling so well in their first year indicates that Detroit's vast researches have for a long time failed to reveal what customers really wanted. Detroit was not convinced that people wanted anything different from what they had been getting until it lost millions of customers to other small-car manufacturers.

How could this unbelievable lag behind consumer wants have been perpetuated for so long? Why did not research reveal consumer preferences before consumers' buying decisions themselves revealed the facts? Is that not what consumer research is for—to find out before the fact what is going to happen? The answer is that Detroit never really researched customers' wants. It only researched their preferences between the kinds of things it had already decided to offer them. For Detroit is mainly product oriented, not customer oriented. To the extent that the customer is recognized as having needs that the manufacturer should try to satisfy, Detroit usually acts as if the job can be done entirely by product changes. Occasionally, attention gets paid to financing, too, but that is done more in order to sell than to enable the customer to buy.

As for taking care of other customer needs, there is not enough being done to write about. The areas of the greatest unsatisfied needs are ignored or, at best, get stepchild attention. These are at the point of sale and on the matter of automotive repair and maintenance. Detroit views these problem areas as being of secondary importance. That is underscored by the fact that the retailing and servicing ends of this industry are neither owned and operated nor controlled by the manufacturers. Once the car is produced, things are pretty much in the dealer's inadequate hands. Illustrative of Detroit's arms-length attitude is the fact that, while servicing holds enormous sales-stimulating, profit-building opportunities, only 57 of Chevrolet's 7,000 dealers provide night maintenance service.

Motorists repeatedly express their dissatisfaction with servicing and their apprehensions about buying cars under the present selling setup. The anxieties and problems they encounter during the auto buying and maintenance processes are probably more intense and widespread today than many years ago. Yet the automobile companies do not seem to listen to or take their cues from the anguished consumer. If they do listen, it must be through the filter of their own preoccupation with production. The marketing effort is still viewed as a necessary consequence of the product—not vice versa, as it should be. That is the legacy of mass production, with its parochial view that profit resides essentially in low-cost full production.

What Ford Put First
The profit lure of mass production obviously has a place in the plans and strategy of business management, but it must always *follow* hard thinking about the customer. This is one of the most important lessons we can learn from the contradictory behavior of Henry Ford. In a sense, Ford was both the most brilliant and the most senseless marketer in American history. He was senseless because he refused to give the customer anything but a black car. He was brilliant because he fashioned a production system designed to fit market needs. We habitually celebrate him for the wrong reason: for his production genius. His real genius was marketing. We think he was able to cut his selling price and therefore sell millions of $500 cars because his invention of the assembly line had reduced the costs. Actually, he invented the assembly line because he had concluded that at $500 he could sell millions of cars. Mass

production was the *result,* not the cause, of his low prices.

Ford emphasized this point repeatedly, but a nation of production-oriented business managers refuses to hear the great lesson he taught. Here is his operating philosophy as he expressed it succinctly:

> Our policy is to reduce the price, extend the operations, and improve the article. You will notice that the reduction of price comes first. We have never considered any costs as fixed. Therefore we first reduce the price to the point where we believe more sales will result. Then we go ahead and try to make the prices. We do not bother about the costs. The new price forces the costs down. The more usual way is to take the costs and then determine the price; and although that method may be scientific in the narrow sense, it is not scientific in the broad sense, because what earthly use is it to know the cost if it tells you that you cannot manufacture at a price at which the article can be sold? But more to the point is the fact that, although one may calculate what a cost is, and of course all of our costs are carefully calculated, no one knows what a cost ought to be. One of the ways of discovering . . . is to name a price so low as to force everybody in the place to the highest point of efficiency. The low price makes everybody dig for profits. We make more discoveries concerning manufacturing and selling under this forced method than by any method of leisurely investigation.[5]

Product Provincialism

The tantalizing profit possibilities of low unit production costs may be the most seriously self-deceiving attitude that can afflict a company, particularly a "growth" company, where an apparently assured expansion of demand already tends to undermine a proper concern for the importance of marketing and the customer.

The usual result of this narrow preoccupation with so-called concrete matters is that instead of growing, the industry declines. It usually means that the product fails to adapt to the constantly changing patterns of consumer needs and tastes, to new and modified marketing institutions and practices, or to product developments in competing or complementary industries. The industry has its eyes so firmly on its own specific product that it does not see how it is being made obsolete.

The classic example of this is the buggy whip industry. No amount of product improvement could stave off its death sentence. But had the industry defined itself as being in the transportation business rather than in the buggy whip business, it might have survived. It would have done what survival always entails—that is, change. Even if it had only defined its business as providing a stimulant or catalyst to an energy source, it might have survived by becoming a manufacturer of, say, fan belts or air cleaners.

What may someday be a still more classic example is, again, the oil industry. Having let others steal marvelous opportunities from it (including natural gas, as already mentioned; missile fuels; and jet engine lubricants), one would expect it to have taken steps never to let that happen again. But this is not the case. We are now seeing extraordinary new developments in fuel systems specifically designed to power automobiles. Not only are these developments concentrated in firms outside the petroleum industry, but petroleum is almost systematically ignoring them, securely content in its wedded bliss to oil. It is the story of the kerosene lamp versus the incandescent lamp all over again. Oil is trying to improve hydrocarbon fuels rather than develop *any* fuels best suited to the needs of their users, whether or not made in different ways and with different raw materials from oil.

Here are some things that nonpetroleum companies are working on. More than a dozen such firms now have advanced working models of energy systems which, when perfected, will replace the internal combustion engine and eliminate the demand for gasoline. The superior merit of each of these systems is their elimination of frequent, time-consuming, and irritating refueling stops. Most of these systems are fuel cells designed to create electrical energy directly from chemicals without combustion. Most of them use chemicals that are not derived from oil—generally, hydrogen and oxygen.

Several other companies have advanced models of electric storage batteries designed to power automobiles. One of these is an aircraft producer that is working jointly with several electric utility companies. The latter hope to use off-peak generating capacity to supply overnight plug-in battery regeneration. Another company, also using the battery approach, is a medium-sized electronics firm with extensive small-battery experience that it developed in connection with its work on hearing aids. It is collaborating with an automobile manufacturer. Recent improvements arising from the need for high-powered miniature power storage plants in rockets have put us within reach of a relatively small battery capable of withstanding great overloads or surges of power. Germanium diode applications and batteries using sintered plate and nickel cadmium techniques promise to make a revolution in our energy sources.

Solar energy conversion systems are also getting increasing attention. One usually cautious Detroit auto executive recently ventured that solar-powered cars might be common by 1980.

As for the oil companies, they are more or less "watching developments," as one research director put it to me. A few are doing a bit of research on fuel cells, but this research is almost always confined to developing cells powered by hydrocarbon chemicals. None of them is enthusiastically researching fuel cells, batteries, or solar power plants. None of them is spending a fraction as much on research in these profoundly important areas as it is on the usual run-of-the-mill things like reducing combustion chamber deposits in gasoline engines. One major integrated petroleum company recently took a tentative look at the fuel cell and concluded that although "the companies actively working on it indicate a belief in ultimate success . . . the timing and magnitude of its impact are too remote to warrant recognition in our forecasts."

One might, of course, ask, Why should the oil companies do anything different? Would not chemical fuel cells, batteries, or solar energy kill the present product lines? The answer is that they would indeed, and that is precisely the reason for the oil firms' having to develop these power units before their competitors do, so they will not be companies without an industry.

Management might be more likely to do what is needed for its own preservation if it thought of itself as being in the energy business. But even that will not be enough if it persists in imprisoning itself in the narrow grip of its tight product orientation. It has to think of itself as taking care of customer needs, not finding, refining, or even selling oil. Once it genuinely thinks of its business as taking care of people's transportation needs, nothing can stop it from creating its own extravagantly profitable growth.

Creative Destruction

Since words are cheap and deeds are dear, it may be appropriate to indicate what this kind of thinking involves and leads to. Let us start at the beginning: the customer. It can be shown that motorists strongly dislike the bother, delay, and experience of buying gasoline. People actually do not buy gasoline. They cannot see it, taste it, feel it, appreciate it, or really test it. What they buy is the right to continue driving their cars. The gas station is like a tax collector to whom people are compelled to pay a periodic toll as the price of using their cars. This makes the gas station a basically unpopular institution. It can never be made popular or pleasant, only less unpopular, less unpleasant.

Reducing its unpopularity completely means eliminating it. Nobody likes a tax collector, not even a pleasantly cheerful one. Nobody likes to interrupt a trip to buy a phantom product, not even from a handsome Adonis or a seductive Venus. Hence, companies that are working on exotic fuel substitutes that will eliminate the need for frequent refueling are heading directly into the outstretched arms of the irritated motorist. They are riding a wave of inevitability, not because they are creating something that is technologically superior or more sophisticated but because they are satisfying a powerful customer need. They are also eliminating noxious odors and air pollution.

Once the petroleum companies recognize the customer-satisfying logic of what another power system can do, they will see that they have no more choice about working on an efficient, long-lasting fuel (or some way of delivering present fuels without bothering the motorist) than the big food chains had a choice about going into the supermarket business or the vacuum tube companies had a choice about making semiconductors. For their own good, the oil firms will have to destroy their own highly profitable assets. No amount of wishful thinking can save them from the necessity of engaging in this form of "creative destruction."

I phrase the need as strongly as this because I think management must make quite an effort to break itself loose from conventional ways. It is all too easy in this day and age for a company or industry to let its sense of purpose become dominated by the economies of full production and to develop a dangerously lopsided product orientation. In short, if management lets itself drift, it invariably drifts in the direction of thinking of itself as producing goods and services, not customer satisfactions. While it probably will not descend to the depths of telling its salespeople, "You get rid of it; we'll worry about profits," it can, without knowing it, be practicing precisely that formula for withering decay. The historic fate of one growth industry after another has been its suicidal product provincialism.

Dangers of R&D

Another big danger to a firm's continued growth arises when top management is wholly transfixed by the profit possibilities of technical research and development. To illustrate, I shall turn first to a new industry—electronics—and then return once more to the oil companies. By comparing a fresh example with a familiar one, I hope to emphasize the prevalence and insidiousness of a hazardous way of thinking.

Marketing Shortchanged

In the case of electronics, the greatest danger that faces the glamorous new companies in this field is not that they do not pay enough attention to research and development but that they pay too much attention to it. And the fact that the fastest-growing electronics firms owe their eminence to their heavy emphasis on technical research is completely beside the point. They have vaulted to affluence on a sudden crest of unusually strong general receptiveness to new technical ideas. Also, their success has been shaped in the virtually guaranteed market of military subsidies and by military orders that in many cases actually preceded the existence of facilities to make the products. Their expansion has, in other words, been almost totally devoid of marketing effort.

Thus, they are growing up under conditions that come dangerously close to creating the illusion that a superior product will sell itself. It is not surprising that, having created a successful company by making a superior product, management continues to be oriented toward the product rather than the people who consume it. It develops the philosophy that continued growth is a matter of continued product innovation and improvement.

A number of other factors tend to strengthen and sustain this belief:

1. Because electronic products are highly complex and sophisticated, managements become top-heavy with engineers and scientists. This creates a selective bias in favor of research and production at the expense of marketing. The organization tends to view itself as making things rather than as satisfying customer needs. Marketing gets treated as a residual activity, "something else" that must be done once the vital job of product creation and production is completed.

2. To this bias in favor of product research, development, and production is added the bias in favor of

dealing with controllable variables. Engineers and scientists are at home in the world of concrete things like machines, test tubes, production lines, and even balance sheets. The abstractions to which they feel kindly are those that are testable or manipulatable in the laboratory or, if not testable, then functional, such as Euclid's axioms. In short, the managements of the new glamour-growth companies tend to favor business activities that lend themselves to careful study, experimentation, and control—the hard, practical realities of the lab, the shop, and the books.

What gets shortchanged are the realities of the *market*. Consumers are unpredictable, varied, fickle, stupid, shortsighted, stubborn, and generally bothersome. This is not what the engineer managers say, but deep down in their consciousness, it is what they believe. And this accounts for their concentration on what they know and what they can control—namely, product research, engineering, and production. The emphasis on production becomes particularly attractive when the product can be made at declining unit costs. There is no more inviting way of making money than by running the plant full blast.

The top-heavy science-engineering-production orientation of so many electronics companies works reasonably well today because they are pushing into new frontiers in which the armed services have pioneered virtually assured markets. The companies are in the felicitous position of having to fill, not find, markets, of not having to discover what the customer needs and wants but of having the customer voluntarily come forward with specific new product demands. If a team of consultants had been assigned specifically to design a business situation calculated to prevent the emergence and development of a customer-oriented marketing viewpoint, it could not have produced anything better than the conditions just described.

Stepchild Treatment

The oil industry is a stunning example of how science, technology, and mass production can divert an entire group of companies from their main task. To the extent the consumer is studied at all (which is not much), the focus is forever on getting information that is designed to help the oil companies improve what they are now doing. They try to discover more convincing advertising themes, more effective sales promotional drives, what the market shares of the various companies are, what people like or dislike about service station dealers and oil companies, and so forth. Nobody seems as interested in probing deeply into the basic human needs that the industry might be trying to satisfy as in probing into the basic properties of the raw material that the companies work with in trying to deliver customer satisfactions.

Basic questions about customers and markets seldom get asked. The latter occupy a stepchild status. They are recognized as existing, as having to be taken care of, but not worth very much real thought or dedicated attention. No oil company gets as excited about the customers in its own backyard as about the oil in the Sahara Desert. Nothing illustrates better the neglect of marketing than its treatment in the industry press.

The centennial issue of the *American Petroleum Institute Quarterly,* published in 1959 to celebrate the discovery of oil in Titusville, Pennsylvania, contained 21 feature articles proclaiming the industry's greatness. Only one of these talked about its achievements in marketing, and that was only a pictorial record of how service station architecture has changed. The issue also contained a special section on "New Horizons," which was devoted to showing the magnificent role oil would play in America's future. Every reference was ebulliently optimistic, never implying once that oil might have some hard competition. Even the reference to atomic energy was a cheerful catalog of how oil would help make atomic energy a success. There was not a single apprehension that the oil industry's affluence might be threatened or a suggestion that one "new horizon" might include new and better ways of serving oil's present customers.

But the most revealing example of the stepchild treatment that marketing gets is still another special series of short articles on "The Revolutionary Potential of Electronics." Under that heading, this list of articles appeared in the table of contents:

- "In the Search for Oil"

- "In Production Operations"

- "In Refinery Processes"

- "In Pipeline Operations"

Significantly, every one of the industry's major functional areas is listed, *except* marketing. Why? Either it is believed that electronics holds no revolutionary potential for petroleum marketing (which is palpably wrong), or the editors forgot to discuss marketing (which is more likely and illustrates its stepchild status).

The order in which the four functional areas are listed also betrays the alienation of the oil industry from the consumer. The industry is implicitly defined as beginning with the search for oil and ending with its distribution from the refinery. But the truth is, it seems to me, that the industry begins with the needs of the customer for its products. From that primal position its definition moves steadily back stream to areas of progressively lesser importance until it finally comes to rest at the search for oil.

The Beginning and End
The view that an industry is a customer-satisfying process, not a goods-producing process, is vital for all businesspeople to understand. An industry begins with the customer and his or her needs, not with a patent, a raw material, or a selling skill. Given the customer's needs, the industry develops backwards, first concerning itself with the physical *delivery* of customer satisfactions. Then it moves back further to *creating* the things by which these satisfactions are in part achieved. How these materials are created is a matter of indifference to the customer, hence the particular form of manufacturing, processing, or what have you cannot be considered as a vital aspect of the industry. Finally, the industry

moves back still further to *finding* the raw materials necessary for making its products.

The irony of some industries oriented toward technical research and development is that the scientists who occupy the high executive positions are totally unscientific when it comes to defining their companies' overall needs and purposes. They violate the first two rules of the scientific method: being aware of and defining their companies' problems and then developing testable hypotheses about solving them. They are scientific only about the convenient things, such as laboratory and product experiments.

The customer (and the satisfaction of his or her deepest needs) is not considered to be "the problem"—not because there is any certain belief that no such problem exists but because an organizational lifetime has conditioned management to look in the opposite direction. Marketing is a stepchild.

I do not mean that selling is ignored. Far from it. But selling, again, is not marketing. As already pointed out, selling concerns itself with the tricks and techniques of getting people to exchange their cash for your product. It is not concerned with the values that the exchange is all about. And it does not, as marketing invariably does, view the entire business process as consisting of a tightly integrated effort to discover, create, arouse, and satisfy customer needs. The customer is somebody "out there" who, with proper cunning, can be separated from his or her loose change.

Actually, not even selling gets much attention in some technologically minded firms. Because there is a virtually guaranteed market for the abundant flow of their new products, they do not actually know what a real market is. It is as if they lived in a planned economy, moving their products routinely from factory to retail outlet. Their successful concentration on products tends to convince them of the soundness of what they have been doing, and they fail to see the gathering clouds over the market.

Less than 75 years ago, American railroads enjoyed a fierce loyalty among astute Wall Streeters. European monarchs invested in them heavily. Eternal wealth was thought to be the benediction for anybody who could scrape together a few thousand dollars to put into rail stocks. No other form of transportation could compete with the railroads in speed, flexibility, durability, economy, and growth potentials.

As Jacques Barzun put it, "By the turn of the century it was an institution, an image of man, a tradition, a code of honor, a source of poetry, a nursery of boyhood desires, a sublimest of toys, and the most solemn machine—next to the funeral hearse—that marks the epochs in man's life."[6]

Even after the advent of automobiles, trucks, and airplanes, the railroad tycoons remained imperturbably self-confident. If you had told them 60 years ago that in 30 years they would be flat on their backs, broke, and pleading for government subsidies, they would have thought you totally demented. Such a future was simply not considered possible. It was not even a discussable subject, or an askable question, or a matter that any sane person would consider worth speculating about. Yet a lot of "insane" notions now have matter-of-fact acceptance—for example, the idea of 100-ton tubes of metal moving smoothly through the air 20,000 feet above the earth, loaded with 100 sane and solid citizens casually drinking martinis—and they have dealt cruel blows to the railroads.

What specifically must other companies do to avoid this fate? What does customer orientation involve? These questions have in part been answered by the preceding examples and analysis. It would take another article to show in detail what is required for specific industries. In any case, it should be obvious that building an effective customer-oriented company involves far more than good intentions or promotional tricks; it involves profound matters of human organization and leadership. For the present, let me merely suggest what appear to be some general requirements.

The Visceral Feel of Greatness

Obviously, the company has to do what survival demands. It has to adapt to the requirements of the market, and it has to do it sooner rather than later. But mere survival is a so-so aspiration. Anybody can survive in some way or other, even the skid row bum. The trick is to survive gallantly, to feel the surging impulse of commercial mastery: not just to experience the sweet smell of success but to have the visceral feel of entrepreneurial greatness.

No organization can achieve greatness without a vigorous leader who is driven onward by a pulsating *will to succeed*. A leader has to have a vision of grandeur, a vision that can produce eager followers in vast numbers. In business, the followers are the customers.

In order to produce these customers, the entire corporation must be viewed as a customer-creating and customer-satisfying organism. Management must think of itself not as producing products but as providing customer-creating value satisfactions. It must push this idea (and everything it means and requires) into every nook and cranny of the organization. It has to do this continuously and with the kind of flair that excites and stimulates the people in it. Otherwise, the company will be merely a series of pigeonholed parts, with no consolidating sense of purpose or direction.

In short, the organization must learn to think of itself not as producing goods or services but as *buying customers,* as doing the things that will make people *want* to do business with it. And the chief executive has the inescapable responsibility for creating this environment, this viewpoint, this attitude, this aspiration. The chief executive must set the company's style, its direction, and its goals. This means knowing precisely where he or she wants to go and making sure the whole organization is enthusiastically aware of where that is. This is a first requisite of leadership, for *unless a leader knows where he is going, any road will take him there.*

If any road is okay, the chief executive might as well pack his attaché case and go fishing. If an organization does not know or care where it is going, it does not need to advertise that fact with a ceremonial figurehead. Everybody will notice it soon enough.

Notes

1. Jacques Barzun, "Trains and the Mind of Man," *Holiday,* February 1960.
2. For more details, see M.M. Zimmerman, *The Super Market: A Revolution in Distribution* (McGraw-Hill, 1955).
3. Ibid., pp. 45–47.
4. John Kenneth Galbraith, *The Affluent Society* (Houghton Mifflin, 1958).
5. Henry Ford, *My Life and Work* (Doubleday, 1923).
6. Barzun, "Trains and the Mind of Man."

THEODORE LEVITT was the Edward W. Carter Professor of Business Administration at Harvard Business School.

Originally published in 1960. Reprint R0407L

Marketing Malpractice

The Cause and the Cure
by Clayton M. Christensen, Scott Cook, and Taddy Hall

THIRTY THOUSAND NEW CONSUMER products are launched each year. But over 90% of them fail—and that's after marketing professionals have spent massive amounts of money trying to understand what their customers want. What's wrong with this picture? Is it that market researchers aren't smart enough? That advertising agencies aren't creative enough? That consumers have become too difficult to understand? We don't think so. We believe, instead, that some of the fundamental paradigms of marketing—the methods that most of us learned to segment markets, build brands, and understand customers—are broken. We're not alone in that judgment. Even Procter & Gamble CEO A.G. Lafley, arguably the best-positioned person in the world to make this call, says, "We need to reinvent the way we market to consumers. We need a new model."

To build brands that mean something to customers, you need to attach them to products that mean something to customers. And to do that, you need to segment markets in ways that reflect how customers actually live their lives. In this article, we will propose a way to reconfigure the principles of market segmentation. We'll describe how to create products that customers will consistently value. And finally, we will describe how new, valuable brands can be built to truly deliver sustained, profitable growth.

Broken Paradigms of Market Segmentation

The great Harvard marketing professor Theodore Levitt used to tell his students, "People don't want to buy a quarter-inch drill. They want a quarter-inch hole!" Every marketer we know agrees with Levitt's insight. Yet these same people segment their markets by type of drill and by price point; they measure market share of drills, not holes; and they benchmark the features and functions of their drill, not their hole, against those of rivals. They then set to work offering more features and functions in the belief that these will translate into better pricing and market share. When marketers do this, they often solve the wrong problems, improving their products in ways that are irrelevant to their customers' needs.

Segmenting markets by type of customer is no better. Having sliced business clients into small, medium, and large enterprises—or having shoehorned consumers into age, gender, or lifestyle brackets—marketers busy

Idea in Brief

Thirty thousand new consumer products hit store shelves each year. Ninety percent of them fail. Why? We're using misguided market-segmentation practices. For instance, we slice markets based on customer type and define the needs of representative customers in those segments. But actual human beings don't behave like statistically average customers. The consequences? We develop new and enhanced products that don't meet real people's needs.

Here's a better way: Instead of trying to understand the "typical" customer, find out what jobs people want to get done. Then develop **purpose brands**: products or services consumers can "hire" to perform those jobs. FedEx, for example, designed its service to perform the "I-need-to-send-this-from-here-to-there-with-perfect-certainty-as-fast-as-possible" job. FedEx was so much more convenient, reliable, and reasonably priced than the alternatives—the U.S. Postal Service or couriers paid to sit on airlines—that businesspeople around the globe started using "FedEx" as a verb.

A clear purpose brand acts as a two-sided compass: One side guides customers to the right products. The other guides your designers, marketers, and advertisers as they develop and market new and improved products. The payoff? Products your customers consistently value—and brands that deliver sustained profitable growth to your company.

themselves with trying to understand the needs of representative customers in those segments and then create products that address those needs. The problem is that customers don't conform their desires to match those of the average consumer in their demographic segment. When marketers design a product to address the needs of a typical customer in a demographically defined segment, therefore, they cannot know whether any specific individual will buy the product—they can

Idea in Practice

To establish, sustain, and extend your purpose brands.

Observe Consumers in Action

By observing and interviewing people as they're using products, identify jobs they want to get done. Then think of new or enhanced offerings that could do the job better.

Example: A fast-food restaurant wanted to improve milk shake sales. A researcher watched customers buying shakes, noting that 40% of shakes were purchased by hurried customers early in the morning and carried out to customers' cars. Interviews revealed that most customers bought shakes to do a similar job: make their commute more interesting, stave off hunger until lunchtime, and give them something they could consume cleanly with one hand. Understanding this job inspired several product-improvement ideas. One example: Move the shake-dispensing machine to the front of the counter and sell customers a prepaid swipe card, so they could dispense shakes themselves and avoid the slow drive-through lane.

Link Products to Jobs Through Advertising

Use advertising to clarify the nature of the job your product performs and to give the product a name that reinforces awareness of its purpose. Savvy ads can even help consumers identify needs they weren't consciously aware of before.

Example: Unilever's Asian operations designed a microwavable soup tailored to

only express a likelihood of purchase in probabilistic terms.

Thus the prevailing methods of segmentation that budding managers learn in business schools and then practice in the marketing departments of good companies are actually a key reason that new product innovation has become a gamble in which the odds of winning are horrifyingly low.

the job of helping office workers boost their energy and productivity in the late afternoon. Called Soupy Snax, the product generated mediocre results. When Unilever renamed it Soupy Snax—4:00 and created ads showing lethargic workers perking up after using the product, ad viewers remarked, "That's what happens to me at 4:00!" Soupy Snax sales soared.

Extend Your Purpose Brand

If you extend your purpose brand onto products that do different jobs—for example, a toothpaste that freshens breath *and* whitens teeth *and* reduces plaque—customers may become confused and lose trust in your brand.

To extend your brand without destroying it:

- **Develop different products that address a common job.** Sony did this with its various generations of Walkman that helped consumers "escape the chaos in my world."

- **Identify new, related jobs and create purpose brands for them.** Marriott International extended its hotel brand, originally built around full-service facilities designed for large meetings, to other types of hotels. Each new purpose brand had a name indicating the job it was designed to do. For instance, Courtyard Marriott was "hired" by individual business travelers seeking a clean, quiet place to get work done in the evening. Residence Inn was hired by longer-term travelers.

There is a better way to think about market segmentation and new product innovation. The structure of a market, seen from the customers' point of view, is very simple: They just need to get things done, as Ted Levitt said. When people find themselves needing to get a job done, they essentially hire products to do that job for them. The marketer's task is therefore to understand what jobs periodically arise in customers' lives for which they might hire products the company could make. If a marketer can understand the job, design a product and associated experiences in purchase and use to do that job, and deliver it in a way that reinforces its intended use, then when customers find themselves needing to get that job done, they will hire that product.

Since most new-product developers don't think in those terms, they've become much too good at creating products that don't help customers do the jobs they need to get done. Here's an all-too-typical example. In the mid-1990s, Scott Cook presided over the launch of a software product called the Quicken Financial Planner, which helped customers create a retirement plan. It flopped. Though it captured over 90% of retail sales in its product category, annual revenue never surpassed $2 million, and it was eventually pulled from the market.

What happened? Was the $49 price too high? Did the product need to be easier to use? Maybe. A more likely explanation, however, is that while the demographics suggested that lots of families needed a financial plan, constructing one actually wasn't a job that most people were looking to do. The fact that they should have a financial plan, or even that they said they should have a plan, didn't matter. In hindsight, the fact that the design team had had trouble finding enough "planners" to fill a focus group should have tipped Cook off. Making it easier and cheaper for customers to do things that they are not trying to do rarely leads to success.

Designing Products That Do the Job

With few exceptions, every job people need or want to do has a social, a functional, and an emotional dimension. If marketers understand each of these dimensions, then they can design a product that's precisely targeted to the job. In other words, the job, not the customer, is the fundamental unit of analysis for a marketer who hopes to develop products that customers will buy.

To see why, consider one fast-food restaurant's effort to improve sales of its milk shakes. (In this example, both the company and the product have been disguised.) Its marketers first defined the market segment by product—milk shakes—and then segmented it further by profiling the demographic and personality characteristics of those customers who frequently bought milk shakes. Next, they invited people who fit this profile to evaluate whether making the shakes thicker, more chocolaty, cheaper, or chunkier would satisfy them better. The panelists gave clear feedback, but the consequent improvements to the product had no impact on sales.

A new researcher then spent a long day in a restaurant seeking to understand the jobs that customers were trying to get done when they hired a milk shake. He chronicled when each milk shake was bought, what other products the customers purchased, whether these consumers were alone or with a group, whether they consumed the shake on the premises or drove off with it, and so on. He was surprised to find that 40% of all milk shakes were purchased in the early morning. Most often, these early-morning customers were alone; they did not buy anything else; and they consumed their shakes in their cars.

The researcher then returned to interview the morning customers as they left the restaurant, shake in hand, in an effort to understand what caused them to hire a milk shake. Most bought it to do a similar job: They faced a long, boring commute and needed something to make the drive more interesting. They weren't yet hungry but knew that they would be by 10 AM; they wanted to consume something now that would stave off hunger until noon. And they faced constraints: They were in a hurry, they were wearing work clothes, and they had (at most) one free hand.

The researcher inquired further: "Tell me about a time when you were in the same situation but you didn't buy a milk shake. What did you buy instead?" Sometimes, he learned, they bought a bagel. But bagels were too dry. Bagels with cream cheese or jam resulted in sticky fingers and gooey steering wheels. Sometimes these commuters bought a banana, but it didn't last long enough to solve the boring-commute problem. Doughnuts didn't carry people past the 10 AM hunger attack. The milk shake, it turned out, did the job better than any of these competitors. It took people 20 minutes to suck the viscous milk shake through the thin straw, addressing the boring-commute problem. They could consume it cleanly with one hand. By 10:00, they felt less hungry than when they tried the alternatives.

It didn't matter much that it wasn't a healthy food, because becoming healthy wasn't essential to the job they were hiring the milk shake to do.

The researcher observed that at other times of the day parents often bought milk shakes, in addition to complete meals, for their children. What job were the parents trying to do? They were exhausted from repeatedly having to say "no" to their kids. They hired milk shakes as an innocuous way to placate their children and feel like loving parents. The researcher observed that the milk shakes didn't do this job very well, though. He saw parents waiting impatiently after they had finished their own meals while their children struggled to suck the thick shakes up through the thin straws.

Customers were hiring milk shakes for two very different jobs. But when marketers had originally asked individual customers who hired a milk shake for either or both jobs which of its attributes they should improve—and when these responses were averaged with those of other customers in the targeted demographic segment—it led to a one-size-fits-none product.

Once they understood the jobs the customers were trying to do, however, it became very clear which improvements to the milk shake would get those jobs done even better and which were irrelevant. How could they tackle the boring-commute job? Make the milk shake even thicker, so it would last longer. And swirl in tiny chunks of fruit, adding a dimension of unpredictability and anticipation to the monotonous morning routine. Just as important, the restaurant chain could deliver the product more effectively by moving the dispensing machine in front of the counter and selling customers a prepaid swipe card so they could dash in, "gas up," and go without getting stuck in the drive-through lane. Addressing the midday and evening job to be done would entail a very different product, of course.

By understanding the job and improving the product's social, functional, and emotional dimensions so that it did the job better, the company's milk shakes would gain share against the real competition—not just competing chains' milk shakes but bananas, boredom, and bagels. This would grow the category, which brings us to an important point: Job-defined markets are generally much larger than product category-defined markets. Marketers who are stuck in the mental trap that equates market size with product categories don't understand whom they are competing against from the customer's point of view.

Notice that knowing how to improve the product did not come from understanding the "typical" customer. It came from understanding the job. Need more evidence?

Pierre Omidyar did not design eBay for the "auction psychographic." He founded it to help people sell personal items. Google was designed for the job of finding information, not for a "search demographic." The unit of analysis in the work that led to Procter & Gamble's stunningly successful Swiffer was the job of cleaning floors, not a demographic or psychographic study of people who mop.

Why do so many marketers try to understand the consumer rather than the job? One reason may be purely historical: In some of the markets in which the tools of modern market research were formulated and tested, such as feminine hygiene or baby care, the job was so closely aligned with the customer demographic that if you understood the customer, you would also understand the job. This coincidence is rare, however. All too frequently, marketers' focus on the customer causes them to target phantom needs.

How a Job Focus Can Grow Product Categories

New growth markets are created when innovating companies design a product and position its brand on a job for which no optimal product yet exists. In fact, companies that historically have segmented and measured the size of their markets by product category generally find that when they instead segment by job, their market is much larger (and their current share of the job is much smaller) than they had thought. This is great news for smart companies hungry for growth.

Understanding and targeting jobs was the key to Sony founder Akio Morita's approach to disruptive innovation. Morita never did conventional market research. Instead, he and his associates spent much of their time watching what people were trying to get done in their lives, then asking themselves whether Sony's electronics miniaturization technology could help them do these things better, easier, and cheaper. Morita would have badly misjudged the size of his market had he simply analyzed trends in the number of tape players being sold before he launched his

Walkman. This should trigger an action item on every marketer's to-do list: Turn off the computer, get out of the office, and observe.

Consider how Church & Dwight used this strategy to grow its baking soda business. The company has produced Arm & Hammer baking soda since the 1860s; its iconic yellow box and Vulcan's hammer-hefting arm have become enduring visual cues for "the standard of purity." In the late 1960s, market research director Barry Goldblatt tells us, management began observational research to understand the diverse circumstances in which consumers found themselves with a job to do where Arm & Hammer could be hired to help. They found a few consumers adding the product to laundry detergent, a few others mixing it into toothpaste, some sprinkling it on the carpet, and still others placing open boxes in the refrigerator. There was a plethora of jobs out there needing to get done, but most customers did not know that they could hire Arm & Hammer baking soda for these cleaning and freshening jobs. The single product just wasn't giving customers the guidance they needed, given the many jobs it could be hired to do.

Today, a family of job-focused Arm & Hammer products has greatly grown the baking soda product category. These jobs include:

- Help my mouth feel fresh and clean (Arm & Hammer Complete Care toothpaste)
- Deodorize my refrigerator (Arm & Hammer Fridge-n-Freezer baking soda)

- Help my underarms stay clean and fresh (Arm & Hammer Ultra Max deodorant)
- Clean and freshen my carpets (Arm & Hammer Vacuum Free carpet deodorizer)
- Deodorize kitty litter (Arm & Hammer Super Scoop cat litter)
- Make my clothes smell fresh (Arm & Hammer Laundry Detergent).

The yellow-box baking soda business is now less than 10% of Arm & Hammer's consumer revenue. The company's share price has appreciated at nearly four times the average rate of its nearest rivals, P&G, Unilever, and Colgate-Palmolive. Although the overall Arm & Hammer brand is valuable in each instance, the key to this extraordinary growth is a set of job-focused products and a communication strategy that help people realize that when they find themselves needing to get one of these jobs done, here is a product that they can trust to do it well.

Building Brands That Customers Will Hire

Sometimes, the discovery that one needs to get a job done is conscious, rational, and explicit. At other times, the job is so much a part of a routine that customers aren't really consciously aware of it. Either way, if consumers are lucky, when they discover the job they need to do, a branded product will exist that is perfectly and unambiguously suited to do it. We call the brand of a

Purpose Brands and Disruptive Innovations

WE HAVE WRITTEN ELSEWHERE about how to harness the potential of disruptive innovations to create growth. Because disruptive innovations are products or services whose performance is not as good as mainstream products, executives of leading companies often hesitate to introduce them for fear of destroying the value of their brands. This fear is generally unfounded, provided that companies attach a unique purpose brand to their disruptive innovations.

Purpose branding has been the key, for example, to Kodak's success with two disruptions. The first was its single-use camera, a classic disruptive technology. Because of its inexpensive plastic lenses, the new camera couldn't take the quality of photographs that a good 35-millimeter camera could produce on Kodak film. The proposition to launch a single-use camera encountered vigorous opposition within Kodak's film division. The corporation finally gave responsibility for the opportunity to a completely different organizational unit, which launched single-use cameras with a purpose brand—the Kodak Fun-Saver. This was a product customers could hire when they needed to save memories of a fun time but had forgotten to bring a camera or didn't want to risk harming their expensive one. Creating a purpose brand for a disruptive job differentiated the product, clarified its

product that is tightly associated with the job for which it is meant to be hired a *purpose brand*.

The history of Federal Express illustrates how successful purpose brands are built. A job had existed practically forever: the I-need-to-send-this-from-here-to-there-with-perfect-certainty-as-fast-as-possible job. Some U.S. customers hired the U.S. Postal Service's airmail to do this job; a few desperate souls paid couriers to sit on airplanes. Others even went so far as to plan

intended use, delighted the customers, and thereby strengthened the endorsing power of the Kodak brand. Quality, after all, can only be measured relative to the job that needs to be done and the alternatives that can be hired to do it. (Sadly, a few years ago, Kodak pushed aside the FunSaver purpose brand in favor of the word "Max," which now appears on its single-use cameras, perhaps to focus on selling film rather than the job the film is for.)

Kodak scored another purpose-branding victory with its disruptive EasyShare digital camera. The company initially had struggled for differentiation and market share in the head-on megapixel and megazoom race against Japanese digital camera makers (all of whom aggressively advertised their corporate brands but had no purpose brands). Kodak then adopted a disruptive strategy that was focused on a job—sharing fun. It made an inexpensive digital camera that customers could slip into a cradle, click "attach" in their computer's e-mail program, and share photos effortlessly with friends and relatives. Sharing fun, not preserving the highest resolution images for posterity, is the job—and Kodak's EasyShare purpose brand guides customers to a product tailored to do that job. Kodak is now the market share leader in digital cameras in the United States.

ahead so they could ship via UPS trucks. But each of these alternatives was kludgy, expensive, uncertain, or inconvenient. Because nobody had yet designed a service to do this job well, the brands of the unsatisfactory alternative services became tarnished when they were hired for this purpose. But after Federal Express designed its service to do that exact job, and did it wonderfully again and again, the FedEx brand began popping into people's minds whenever they needed to get that job done. FedEx became a purpose brand—in fact, it became a verb in the international language of business that is inextricably linked with that specific job. It is a very valuable brand as a result.

Most of today's great brands—Crest, Starbucks, Kleenex, eBay, and Kodak, to name a few—started out as just this kind of purpose brand. The product did the job, and customers talked about it. This is how brand equity is built.

Brand equity can be destroyed when marketers don't tie the brand to a purpose. When they seek to build a general brand that does not signal to customers when they should and should not buy the product, marketers run the risk that people might hire their product to do a job it was not designed to do. This causes customers to distrust the brand—as was the case for years with the post office.

A clear purpose brand is like a two-sided compass. One side guides customers to the right products. The other side guides the company's product designers, marketers, and advertisers as they develop and market improved and new versions of their products. A good purpose brand clarifies which features and functions are relevant to the job and which potential improvements will prove irrelevant. The price premium that the brand commands is the wage that customers are willing to pay the brand for providing this guidance on both sides of the compass.

The need to feel a certain way—to feel macho, sassy, pampered, or prestigious—is a job that arises in many of our lives on occasion. When we find ourselves needing to do one of these jobs, we can hire a branded product whose purpose is to provide such feelings. Gucci, Absolut, Montblanc, and Virgin, for example, are purpose brands. They link customers who have one of these jobs to do with experiences in purchase and use that do those jobs well. These might be called aspirational jobs. In some aspirational situations, it is the brand itself, more than the functional dimensions of the product, that gets the job done.

The Role of Advertising

Much advertising is wasted in the mistaken belief that it alone can build brands. Advertising cannot build brands, but it can tell people about an existing branded product's ability to do a job well. That's what the managers at Unilever's Asian operations found out when they identified an important job that arose in the lives of many office workers at around 4:00 in the afternoon. Drained of physical and emotional energy, people still had to get a lot done before their workday ended. They needed something to boost their productivity, and they were hiring a range of caffeinated drinks, candy bars, stretch breaks, and conversation to do this job, with mixed results.

Unilever designed a microwavable soup whose properties were tailored to that job—quick to fix, nutritious but not too filling, it can be consumed at your desk but gives you a bit of a break when you go to heat it up. It was launched into the workplace under the descriptive brand Soupy Snax. The results were mediocre. On a hunch, the brand's managers then relaunched the product with advertisements showing lethargic workers perking up after using the product and renamed the brand Soupy Snax—4:00. The reaction of people who saw the advertisements was, "That's exactly what happens to me at 4:00!" They needed something to help them consciously discover both the job and the product they could hire to do it. The tagline and ads transformed a brand that had been a simple description of a product into a purpose brand that clarified the nature of the job and the product that was designed to do it, and the product has become very successful.

Note the role that advertising played in this process. Advertising clarified the nature of the job and helped more people realize that they had the job to do. It informed people that there was a product designed to do that job and gave the product a name people could remember. Advertising is not a substitute for designing products that do specific jobs and ensuring that improvements in their features and functions are relevant to that job. The fact is that most great brands were built before their owners started advertising. Think of Disney, Harley-Davidson, eBay, and Google. Each brand developed a sterling reputation before much was spent on advertising.

Advertising that attempts to short-circuit this process and build, as if from scratch, a brand that people will trust is a fool's errand. Ford, Nissan, Macy's, and many other companies invest hundreds of millions to keep the corporate name or their products' names in the general consciousness of the buying public. Most of these companies' products aren't designed to do specific jobs and therefore aren't usually differentiated from the competition. These firms have few purpose brands in their portfolios and no apparent strategies to create them. Their managers are unintentionally transferring billions in profits to branding agencies in the vain hope that they can buy their way to glory. What is worse, many companies have decided that building new brands is so expensive they will no longer do so. Brand building by advertising is indeed prohibitively expensive. But that's because it's the wrong way to build a brand.

Marketing mavens are fond of saying that brands are hollow words into which meaning gets stuffed. Beware. Executives who think that brand advertising is an effective mechanism for stuffing meaning into some word they have chosen to be their brand generally succeed in stuffing it full of vagueness. The ad agencies and media companies win big in this game, but the companies whose brands are getting stuffed generally find themselves trapped in an expensive, endless arms race with competitors whose brands are comparably vague.

The exceptions to this brand-building rule are the purpose brands for aspirational jobs, where the brand must be built through images in advertising. The method for brand building that is appropriate for these jobs, however, has been wantonly and wastefully misapplied to the rest of the world of branding.

Extending—or Destroying—Brand Equity

Once a strong purpose brand has been created, people within the company inevitably want to leverage it by applying it to other products. Executives should consider these proposals carefully. There are rules about the types of extensions that will reinforce the brand—and the types that will erode it.

If a company chooses to extend a brand onto other products that can be hired to do the same job, it can do so without concern that the extension will compromise what the brand does. For example, Sony's portable CD player, although a different product than its original Walkman-branded radio and cassette players, was positioned on the same job (the help-me-escape-the-chaos-in-my-world job). So the new product caused the Walkman brand to pop even more instinctively into customers' minds when they needed to get that job done. Had Sony not been asleep at the switch, a Walkman-branded MP3 player would have further enhanced this purpose brand. It might even have kept Apple's iPod purpose brand from preempting that job.

The fact that purpose brands are job specific means that when a purpose brand is extended onto products that target different jobs, it will lose its clear meaning as a purpose brand and develop a different character instead—an *endorser brand*. An endorser brand can impart a general sense of quality, and it thereby creates some value in a marketing equation. But general endorser brands lose their ability to guide people who have a particular job to do to products that were designed to do it. Without appropriate guidance, customers will begin using endorser-branded products to do jobs they weren't designed to do. The resulting bad experience will cause customers to distrust the brand. Hence, the value of an endorser brand will erode unless the company adds a second word to its brand architecture—a purpose brand alongside the endorser brand. Different jobs demand different purpose brands.

Marriott International's executives followed this principle when they sought to leverage the Marriott brand to address different jobs for which a hotel might be hired. Marriott had built its hotel brand around full-service facilities that were good to hire for large meetings. When it decided to extend its brand to other types of hotels, it adopted a two-word brand architecture that appended to the Marriott endorsement a purpose brand for each of the different jobs its new hotel chains were intended to do. Hence, individual business travelers who need to hire a clean, quiet place to get work done in the evening can hire Courtyard by Marriott—the hotel designed by business travelers for business travelers. Longer-term travelers can hire Residence Inn by Marriott, and so on. Even though these hotels were not constructed and decorated to the same premium standard as full-service Marriott hotels, the new chains actually reinforce the endorser qualities of the Marriott brand because they do the jobs well that they are hired to do.

Milwaukee Electric Tool has built purpose brands with two—and only two—of the products in its line of power tools. The Milwaukee Sawzall is a reciprocating saw that tradesmen hire when they need to cut through a wall quickly and aren't sure what's under the surface. Plumbers hire Milwaukee's Hole Hawg, a right-angle drill, when they need to drill a hole in a tight space. Competitors like Black & Decker, Bosch, and Makita offer reciprocating saws and right-angle drills with comparable performance and price, but none of them has a purpose brand that pops into a tradesman's mind when he has one of these jobs to do. Milwaukee has owned more than 80% of these two job markets for decades.

Interestingly, Milwaukee offers under its endorser brand a full range of power tools, including circular saws, pistol-grip drills, sanders, and jigsaws. While the durability and relative price of these products are comparable to those of the Sawzall and Hole Hawg, Milwaukee has not built purpose brands for any of these other products. The market share of each is in the low single digits—a testament to the clarifying value of purpose brands versus the general connotation of quality that endorser brands confer. Indeed, a clear purpose brand is usually a more formidable competitive barrier than superior product performance—because competitors can copy performance much more easily than they can copy purpose brands.

The tribulations and successes of P&G's Crest brand is a story of products that ace the customer job, lose their focus, and then bounce back to become strong purpose brands again. Introduced in the mid-1950s, Crest was a classic disruptive technology. Its Fluoristan-reinforced toothpaste made cavity-preventing fluoride treatments cheap and easy to apply at home, replacing an expensive and inconvenient trip to the dentist. Although P&G could have positioned the new product under its existing toothpaste brand, Gleem, its managers chose instead to build a new purpose brand, Crest, which was uniquely positioned on a job. Mothers who wanted to prevent cavities in their children's teeth knew when they saw or heard the word "Crest" that this product was designed to do that job. Because it did the job so well, mothers grew to trust the product and in fact became suspicious of the ability of products without the Crest brand to do that job. This unambiguous association made it a very valuable brand, and Crest passed all its U.S. rivals to become the clear market leader in toothpaste for a generation.

But one cannot sustain victory by standing still. Competitors eventually copied Crest's cavity prevention abilities, turning cavity prevention into a commodity. Crest lost share as competitors innovated in other areas, including flavor, mouthfeel, and commonsense ingredients like baking soda. P&G began copying and advertising these attributes. But unlike Marriott, P&G did not append purpose brands to the general endorsement of Crest, and the brand began losing its distinctiveness.

At the end of the 1990s, new Crest executives brought two disruptions to market, each with its own clear purpose brand. They acquired a start-up named Dr. John's and rebranded its flagship electric toothbrush as the Crest SpinBrush, which they sold for $5—far below the price of competitors' models of the time. They also launched Crest Whitestrips, which allowed people to whiten their teeth at home for a mere $25, far less than dentists charged. With these purpose-branded innovations, Crest generated substantial new growth and regained share leadership in the entire tooth care category.

The exhibit "Extending brands without destroying them" diagrams the two ways marketers can extend a

Extending brands without destroying them

There are only two ways: Marketers can develop different products that address a common job, as Sony did with its various generations of Walkman. Or, like Marriott and Milwaukee, they can identify new, related jobs and create new purpose brands that benefit from the "endorser" quality of the original brand.

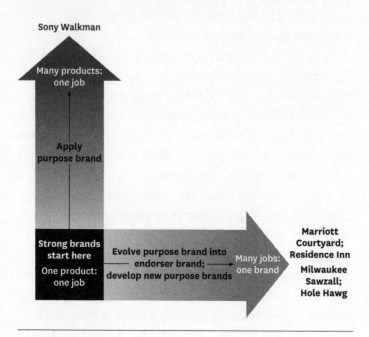

purpose brand without eroding its value. The first option is to move up the vertical axis by developing different products that address a common job. This is what Sony did with its Walkman portable CD player. When Crest was still a clear purpose brand, P&G could have gone this route by, say, introducing a Crest-brand fluoride mouth rinse. The brand would have retained its clarity of purpose. But P&G did not, allowing Johnson & Johnson to insert yet another brand, ACT (its own fluoride mouth rinse), into the cavity-prevention job space. Because P&G pursued the second option, extending its brand along the horizontal axis to other jobs (whitening, breath freshening, and so on), the purpose brand morphed into an endorser brand.

Why Strong Purpose Brands Are So Rare

Given the power that purpose brands have in creating opportunities for differentiation, premium pricing, and growth, isn't it odd that so few companies have a deliberate strategy for creating them?

Consider the automobile industry. There are a significant number of different jobs that people who purchase cars need to get done, but only a few companies have staked out any of these job markets with purpose brands. Range Rover (until recently, at least) was a clear and valuable purpose brand (the take-me-anywhere-with-total-dependability job). The Volvo brand is positioned on the safety job. Porsche, BMW, Mercedes, Bentley, and Rolls-Royce are associated with various aspirational jobs. The Toyota endorser brand has earned the connotation of reliability. But for so much of the rest? It's hard to know what they mean.

To illustrate: Clayton Christensen recently needed to deliver on a long-promised commitment to buy a car as a college graduation gift for his daughter Annie. There were functional and emotional dimensions to the job. The car needed to be stylish and fun to drive, to be sure. But even more important, as his beloved daughter was venturing off into the cold, cruel world, the big job Clay needed to get done was to know that she was safe and for his sweet Annie to be reminded frequently, as she owned, drove, and serviced the car, that her dad loves and cares for her. A hands-free telephone in the car would be a must, not an option. A version of GM's OnStar service, which called not just the police but Clay in the event of an accident, would be important. A system that reminded the occasionally absentminded Annie when she needed to have the car serviced would take a load off her dad's mind. If that service were delivered as a prepaid gift from her father, it would take another load off Clay's mind because he, too, is occasionally absentminded. Should Clay have hired a Taurus, Escape, Cavalier, Neon, Prizm, Corolla, Camry, Avalon, Sentra, Civic, Accord, Senator, Sonata, or something else? The billions of dollars that automakers spent advertising these brands, seeking somehow to create subtle differentiations in image, helped Clay not at all. Finding the best package to hire was very time-consuming and inconvenient, and the resulting product did the job about as unsatisfactorily as the milk shake had done, a few years earlier.

Focusing a product and its brand on a job creates differentiation. The rub, however, is that when a company communicates the job a branded product was designed to do perfectly, it is also communicating what jobs the product should not be hired to do. Focus is scary—at least the carmakers seem to think so. They deliberately create words as brands that have no meaning in any language, with no tie to any job, in the myopic hope that each individual model will be hired by every customer for every job. The results of this strategy speak for themselves. In the face of compelling evidence that purpose-branded products that do specific jobs well command premium pricing and compete in markets that are much larger than those defined by product categories, the automakers' products are substantially undifferentiated, the average subbrand commands less than a 1% market share, and most automakers are losing money. Somebody gave these folks the wrong recipe for prosperity.

Executives everywhere are charged with generating profitable growth. Rightly, they believe that brands are the vehicles for meeting their growth and profit targets. But success in brand building remains rare. Why? Not for lack of effort or resources. Nor for lack of opportunity in the marketplace. The root problem is that the theories in practice for market segmentation and brand building are riddled with flawed assumptions. Lafley is right. The model is broken. We've tried to illustrate a way out of the death spiral of serial product failure, missed opportunity, and squandered wealth. Marketers who choose to break with the broken past will be rewarded not only with successful brands but with profitably growing businesses as well.

CLAYTON M. CHRISTENSEN is the Robert and Jane Cizik Professor of Business Administration at Harvard Business School. **SCOTT COOK** is the chairman of Intuit, based in California. **TADDY HALL** is the chief strategy officer of the Advertising Research Foundation in New York.

Originally published in December 2005. Reprint R0512D

The Brand Report Card

by Kevin Lane Keller

BUILDING AND PROPERLY MANAGING BRAND equity has become a priority for companies of all sizes, in all types of industries, in all types of markets. After all, from strong brand equity flow customer loyalty and profits. The rewards of having a strong brand are clear.

The problem is, few managers are able to step back and assess their brand's particular strengths and weaknesses objectively. Most have a good sense of one or two areas in which their brand may excel or may need help. But if pressed, many (understandably) would find it difficult even to identify all of the factors they should be considering. When you're immersed in the day-to-day management of a brand, it's not easy to keep in perspective all the parts that affect the whole.

In this article, I'll identify the ten characteristics that the world's strongest brands share and construct a brand report card—a systematic way for managers to think about how to grade their brand's performance for each of those characteristics. The report card can help you identify areas that need improvement, recognize areas in which your brand is strong, and learn more about how your particular brand is configured. Constructing similar report cards for your competitors can give you a clearer picture of their strengths and weaknesses. One caveat: Identifying weak spots for your brand doesn't necessarily mean identifying areas that need more attention. Decisions that might seem straightforward—"We haven't paid much attention to innovation: let's direct more resources toward R&D"—can sometimes prove to be serious mistakes if they undermine another characteristic that customers value more.

The Top Ten Traits

The world's strongest brands share these ten attributes.

The brand excels at delivering the benefits customers truly desire

Why do customers really buy a product? Not because the product is a collection of attributes but because those attributes, together with the brand's image, the service, and many other tangible and intangible factors, create an attractive whole. In some cases, the whole isn't even something that customers know or can say they want.

Consider Starbucks. It's not just a cup of coffee. In 1983, Starbucks was a small Seattle-area coffee retailer. Then while on vacation in Italy, Howard Schultz, now Starbucks chairman, was inspired by the romance and the sense of community he felt in Italian coffee bars and

Idea in Brief

It sounds simple: boost your brand equity, and watch profits soar. But many companies stumble in trying to manage their brands' performance.

Consider Levi-Strauss. In the mid-1990s, it launched a brand-equity measurement system that suggested the appeal of its flagship 501 jeans was slipping. But its response to that data was flawed: the company took too long, and spent too little, to mount a marketing campaign that would restore its brand equity. Worse, Levi-Strauss's advertising messages to its target youth market missed their mark. Its market share shriveled.

To strengthen your brand, Keller suggests using a **brand report card**—a tool showing how your brand stacks up on the 10 traits shared by the world's strongest brands. For example, how well does your brand deliver benefits consumers truly desire? How strongly have you positioned it against rivals? How consistent are your marketing messages about your brand?

Use the brand report card, and you identify the actions needed to maximize your brand equity. Your reward? Customers' enduring devotion—and the profits that come with it.

---

coffee houses. The culture grabbed him, and he saw an opportunity.

"It seemed so obvious," Schultz says in the 1997 book he wrote with Dori Jones Yang, *Pour Your Heart Into It*. "Starbucks sold great coffee beans, but we didn't serve coffee by the cup. We treated coffee as produce, something to be bagged and sent home with the groceries. We stayed one big step away from the heart and soul of what coffee has meant throughout centuries."

And so Starbucks began to focus its efforts on building a coffee bar culture, opening coffee houses like those in Italy. Just as important, the company maintained control over the coffee from start to finish—from the selection

Idea in Practice

Grade Your Brand

Keller recommends assessing your brand on the following attributes:

Your brand	Which means...	Example...
1. Delivers benefits customers desire.	It creates an engaging customer experience.	Starbucks delivers the romance and sense of community defining Italian coffee bars and appeals to all senses—not just taste.
2. Stays relevant.	Elements of the brand, such as the type of person who uses the brand, are modified to fit the times.	In marketing its razor blades, Gillette tweaks images of men at work and play to reflect contemporary trends.
3. Is priced based on consumers' perceptions of the brand's value.	The nature of the product—for example, premium versus household staple—should influence price.	Through "everyday low pricing," Procter & Gamble aligned its prices with consumer perceptions of its products as household staples.
4. Is properly positioned.	It clearly communicates its similarities to and differences from competing brands.	Visa labels its cards "Gold" and "Platinum" to equate its status with American Express cards. But it also showcases its cards' superiority through ads featuring desirable locations that don't accept American Express.
5. Is consistent.	Marketing communications don't send conflicting messages over time.	Michelob's market share shriveled over an 18-year period characterized by inconsistent advertising about when customers should drink their beer.

6. Fits sensibly into your brand portfolio.	Brands work logically together.	Clothing retailer Gap Inc.'s Old Navy brand targets the broad mass market, the Gap brand covers basic style-and-quality terrain, and the Banana Republic brand anchors the high-end market.
7. Has an integrated marketing strategy.	All marketing activities and channels communicate the same messages about the brand, solidifying the brand's identity.	Coca-Cola's logo, promotions, corporate sponsorship, and interactive Web site all reinforce the company's key values, such as "originality" and "classic refreshment."
8. Has meanings that managers understand.	Managers know consumers' different perceptions of the brand.	Gillette protects the brand identity for its traditional manual razors by marketing its electric razors under the separate Braun name.
9. Receives sustained support.	Companies consistently invest in building and maintaining brand awareness.	A consumer products company continues its advertising and marketing efforts even after building a positive image in consumers' minds.
10. Is constantly monitored.	Companies use a formal brand-equity-management system.	After Disney's brand audit revealed that consumers resented excessive exposure of the Disney characters, the company decided not to co-brand a mutual fund.

and procurement of the beans to their roasting and blending to their ultimate consumption. The extreme vertical integration has paid off. Starbucks locations thus far have successfully delivered superior benefits to customers by appealing to all five senses—through the enticing aroma of the beans, the rich taste of the coffee, the product displays and attractive artwork adorning the walls, the contemporary music playing in the background, and even the cozy, clean feel of the tables and chairs. The company's startling success is evident: The average Starbucks customer visits a store 18 times a month and spends $3.50 a visit. The company's sales and profits have each grown more than 50% annually through much of the 1990s.

The brand stays relevant

In strong brands, brand equity is tied both to the actual quality of the product or service and to various intangible factors. Those intangibles include "user imagery" (the type of person who uses the brand); "usage imagery" (the type of situations in which the brand is used); the type of personality the brand portrays (sincere, exciting, competent, rugged); the feeling that the brand tries to elicit in customers (purposeful, warm); and the type of relationship it seeks to build with its customers (committed, casual, seasonal). Without losing sight of their core strengths, the strongest brands stay on the leading edge in the product arena and tweak their intangibles to fit the times.

Gillette, for example, pours millions of dollars into R&D to ensure that its razor blades are as technologically advanced as possible, calling attention to major advances through subbrands (Trac II, Atra, Sensor, Mach3) and signaling minor improvements with modifiers (AtraPlus, SensorExcel). At the same time, Gillette has created a consistent, intangible sense of product superiority with its long-running ads, "The best a man can be," which are tweaked through images of men at work and at play that have evolved over time to reflect contemporary trends.

These days, images can be tweaked in many ways other than through traditional advertising, logos, or slogans. "Relevance" has a deeper, broader meaning in today's market. Increasingly, consumers' perceptions of a company as a whole and its role in society affect a brand's strength as well. Witness corporate brands that very visibly support breast cancer research or current educational programs of one sort or another.

The pricing strategy is based on consumers' perceptions of value

The right blend of product quality, design, features, costs, and prices is very difficult to achieve but well worth the effort. Many managers are woefully unaware of how price can and should relate to what customers think of a product, and they therefore charge too little or too much.

For example, in implementing its value-pricing strategy for the Cascade automatic-dishwashing detergent brand, Procter & Gamble made a cost-cutting change in its formulation that had an adverse effect on the product's performance under certain—albeit somewhat atypical—water conditions. Lever Brothers quickly

Rating Your Brand

RATE YOUR BRAND ON a scale of one to ten (one being extremely poor and ten being extremely good) for each characteristic below. Then create a bar chart that reflects the scores. Use the bar chart to generate discussion among all those individuals who participate in the management of your brands. Looking at the results in that manner should help you identify areas that need improvement, recognize areas in which you excel, and learn more about how your particular brand is configured.

It can also be helpful to create a report card and chart for competitors' brands simply by rating those brands based on your own perceptions, both as a competitor and as a consumer. As an outsider, you may know more about how their brands are received in the marketplace than they do.

Keep that in mind as you evaluate your own brand. Try to look at it through the eyes of consumers' rather than through your own knowledge of budgets, teams, and time spent on various initiatives.

- **The brand excels at delivering the benefits customers truly desire.** Have you attempted to uncover unmet consumer needs and wants? By what methods? Do you focus relentlessly on maximizing your customers' product and service experiences? Do you have a system in place for getting comments from customers to the people who can effect change?

countered, attacking Cascade's core equity of producing "virtually spotless" dishes out of the dishwasher. In response, P&G immediately returned to the brand's old formulation. The lesson to P&G and others is that value pricing should not be adopted at the expense of essential brand-building activities.

By contrast, with its well-known shift to an "everyday low pricing" (EDLP) strategy, Procter & Gamble did

- **The brand stays relevant.** Have you invested in product improvements that provide better value for your customers? Are you in touch with your customers' tastes? With the current market conditions? With new trends as they apply to your offering? Are your marketing decisions based on your knowledge of the above?

- **The pricing strategy is based on consumers' perceptions of value.** Have you optimized price, cost, and quality to meet or exceed customers' expectations? Do you have a system in place to monitor customers' perceptions of your brand's value? Have you estimated how much value your customers believe the brand adds to your product?

- **The brand is properly positioned.** Have you established necessary and competitive points of parity with competitors? Have you established desirable and deliverable points of difference?

- **The brand is consistent.** Are you sure that your marketing programs are not sending conflicting messages and that they haven't done so over time? Conversely, are you adjusting your programs to keep current?

- **The brand portfolio and hierarchy make sense.** Can the corporate brand create a seamless umbrella for all the brands in the

(continued)

successfully align its prices with consumer perceptions of its products' value while maintaining acceptable profit levels. In fact, in the fiscal year after Procter & Gamble switched to EDLP (during which it also worked very hard to streamline operations and lower costs), the company reported its highest profit margins in 21 years.

Rating Your Brand (continued)

portfolio? Do the brands in that portfolio hold individual niches? How extensively do the brands overlap? In what areas? Conversely, do the brands maximize market coverage? Do you have a brand hierarchy that is well thought out and well understood?

- **The brand makes use of and coordinates a full repertoire of marketing activities to build equity.** Have you chosen or designed your brand name, logo, symbol, slogan, packaging, signage, and so forth to maximize brand awareness? Have you implemented integrated push and pull marketing activities that target both distributors and customers? Are you aware of all the marketing activities that involve your brand? Are the people managing each activity aware of one another? Have you capitalized on the unique capabilities of each communication option while ensuring that the meaning of the brand is consistently represented?

- **The brand's managers understand what the brand means to consumers.** Do you know what customers like and don't like about a brand? Are you aware of all the core associations people make with your brand, whether intentionally created by your

---

The brand is properly positioned

Brands that are well positioned occupy particular niches in consumers' minds. They are similar to and different from competing brands in certain reliably identifiable ways. The most successful brands in this regard keep up with competitors by creating *points of parity* in those areas where competitors are trying to find an advantage while at the same time creating *points of difference* to achieve advantages over competitors in some other areas.

The Mercedes-Benz and Sony brands, for example, hold clear advantages in product superiority and match

company or not? Have you created detailed, research-driven portraits of your target customers? Have you outlined customer-driven boundaries for brand extensions and guidelines for marketing programs?

- **The brand is given proper support, and that support is sustained over the long run.** Are the successes or failures of marketing programs fully understood before they are changed? Is the brand given sufficient R&D support? Have you avoided the temptation to cut back marketing support for the brand in reaction to a downturn in the market or a slump in sales?

- **The company monitors sources of brand equity.** Have you created a brand charter that defines the meaning and equity of the brand and how it should be treated? Do you conduct periodic brand audits to assess the health of your brand and to set strategic direction? Do you conduct routine tracking studies to evaluate current market performance? Do you regularly distribute brand equity reports that summarize all relevant research and information to assist marketers in making decisions? Have you assigned explicit responsibility for monitoring and preserving brand equity?

---

competitors' level of service. Saturn and Nordstrom lead their respective packs in service and hold their own in quality. Calvin Klein and Harley-Davidson excel at providing compelling user and usage imagery while offering adequate or even strong performance.

Visa is a particularly good example of a brand whose managers understand the positioning game. In the 1970s and 1980s, American Express maintained the high-profile brand in the credit card market through a series of highly effective marketing programs. Trumpeting that "membership has its privileges," American Express came to signify status, prestige, and quality.

In response, Visa introduced the Gold and the Platinum cards and launched an aggressive marketing campaign to build up the status of its cards to match the American Express cards. It also developed an extensive merchant delivery system to differentiate itself on the basis of superior convenience and accessibility. Its ad campaigns showcased desirable locations such as famous restaurants, resorts, and events that did not accept American Express while proclaiming, "Visa. It's everywhere you want to be." The aspirational message cleverly reinforced both accessibility and prestige and helped Visa stake out a formidable position for its brand. Visa became the consumer card of choice for family and personal shopping, for personal travel and entertainment, and even for international travel, a former American Express stronghold.

Of course, branding isn't static, and the game is even more difficult when a brand spans many product categories. The mix of points of parity and point of difference that works for a brand in one category may not be quite right for the same brand in another.

The brand is consistent
Maintaining a strong brand means striking the right balance between continuity in marketing activities and the kind of change needed to stay relevant. By continuity, I mean that the brand's image doesn't get muddled or lost in a cacophony of marketing efforts that confuse customers by sending conflicting messages.

Just such a fate befell the Michelob brand. In the 1970s, Michelob ran ads featuring successful young professionals that confidently proclaimed, "Where you're going, it's Michelob." The company's next ad campaign trumpeted, "Weekends were made for Michelob." Later, in an attempt to bolster sagging sales, the theme was switched to "Put a little weekend in your week." In the mid-1980s, managers launched a campaign telling consumers that "The night belongs to Michelob." Then in 1994 we were told, "Some days are better than others," which went on to explain that "A special day requires a special beer." That slogan was subsequently changed to "Some days were made for Michelob."

Pity the poor consumers. Previous advertising campaigns simply required that they look at their calendars or out a window to decide whether it was the right time to drink Michelob; by the mid-1990s, they had to figure out exactly what kind of day they were having as well. After receiving so many different messages, consumers could hardly be blamed if they had no idea when they were supposed to drink the beer. Predictably, sales suffered. From a high in 1980 of 8.1 million barrels, sales dropped to just 1.8 million barrels by 1998.

The brand portfolio and hierarchy make sense
Most companies do not have only one brand; they create and maintain different brands for different market segments. Single product lines are often sold under different brand names, and different brands within a company hold different powers. The corporate, or comanywide, brand acts as an umbrella. A second brand name under

that umbrella might be targeted at the family market. A third brand name might nest one level below the family brand and appeal to boys, for example, or be used for one type of product.

Brands at each level of the hierarchy contribute to the overall equity of the portfolio through their individual ability to make consumers aware of the various products and foster favorable associations with them. At the same time, though, each brand should have its own boundaries; it can be dangerous to try to cover too much ground with one brand or to overlap two brands in the same portfolio.

The Gap's brand portfolio provides maximum market coverage with minimal overlap. Banana Republic anchors the high end, the Gap covers the basic style-and-quality terrain, and Old Navy taps into the broader mass market. Each brand has a distinct image and its own sources of equity.

BMW has a particularly well-designed and implemented hierarchy. At the corporate brand level, BMW pioneered the luxury sports sedan category by combining seemingly incongruent style and performance considerations. BMW's clever advertising slogan, "The ultimate driving machine," reinforces the dual aspects of this image and is applicable to all cars sold under the BMW name. At the same time, BMW created well-differentiated subbrands through its 3, 5, and 7 series, which suggest a logical order and hierarchy of quality and price.

General Motors, by contrast, still struggles with its brand portfolio and hierarchy. In the early 1920s, Alfred

P. Sloan decreed that his company would offer "a car for every purse and purpose." This philosophy led to the creation of the Cadillac, Oldsmobile, Buick, Pontiac, and Chevrolet divisions. The idea was that each division would appeal to a unique market segment on the basis of price, product design, user imagery, and so forth. Through the years, however, the marketing overlap among the five main GM divisions increased, and the divisions' distinctiveness diminished. In the mid-1980s, for example, the company sold a single body type (the J-body) modified only slightly for the five different brand names. In fact, advertisements for Cadillac in the 1980s actually stated that "motors for a Cadillac may come from other divisions, including Buick and Oldsmobile."

In the last ten years, the company has attempted to sharpen the divisions' blurry images by repositioning each brand. Chevrolet has been positioned as the value-priced, entry-level brand. Saturn represents no-haggle customer-oriented service. Pontiac is meant to be the sporty, performance-oriented brand for young people. Oldsmobile is the brand for larger, medium-priced cars. Buick is the premium, "near luxury" brand. And Cadillac, of course, is still the top of the line. Yet the goal remains challenging. The financial performance of Pontiac and Saturn has improved. But the top and bottom lines have never regained the momentum they had years ago. Consumers remain confused about what the brands stand for, in sharp contrast to the clearly focused images of competitors like Honda and Toyota.

The brand makes use of and coordinates a full repertoire of marketing activities to build equity

At its most basic level, a brand is made up of all the marketing elements that can be trademarked—logos, symbols, slogans, packaging, signage, and so on. Strong brands mix and match these elements to perform a number of brand-related functions, such as enhancing or reinforcing consumer awareness of the brand or its image and helping to protect the brand both competitively and legally.

Managers of the strongest brands also appreciate the specific roles that different marketing activities can play in building brand equity. They can, for example provide detailed product information. They can show consumers how and why a product is used, by whom, where, and when. They can associate a brand with a person, place, or thing to enhance or refine its image.

Some activities, such as traditional advertising, lend themselves best to "pull" functions—those meant to create consumer demand for a given product. Others, like trade promotions, work best as "push" programs—those designed to help push the product through distributors. When a brand makes good use of all its resources and also takes particular care to ensure that the essence of the brand is the same in all activities, it is hard to beat.

Coca-Cola is one of the best examples. The brand makes excellent use of many kinds of marketing activities. These include media advertising (such as the global "Always Coca-Cola" campaign); promotions (the recent effort focused on the return of the popular contour bottle, for example); and sponsorship (its extensive involvement with the Olympics). They also include direct response (the Coca-Cola catalog, which sells licensed Coke merchandise) and interactive media (the company's Web site, which offers, among other things, games, a trading post for collectors of Coke memorabilia, and a virtual look at the World of Coca-Cola museum in Atlanta). Through it all, the company always reinforces its key values of "originality," "classic refreshment," and so on. The brand is always the hero in Coca-Cola advertising.

The brand's managers understand what the brand means to consumers

Managers of strong brands appreciate the totality of their brand's image—that is, all the different perceptions, beliefs, attitudes, and behaviors customers associate with their brand, whether created intentionally by the company or not. As a result, managers are able to make decisions regarding the brand with confidence. If it's clear what customers like and don't like about a brand, and what core associations are linked to the brand, then it should also be clear whether any given action will dovetail nicely with the brand or create friction.

The Bic brand illustrates the kinds of problems that can arise when managers don't fully understand their brand's meaning. By emphasizing the convenience of inexpensive, disposable products, the French company Société Bic was able to create a market for nonrefillable ballpoint pens in the late 1950s, disposable cigarette lighters in the early 1970s, and disposable razors in the early 1980s. But in 1989, when Bic tried the same strategy with perfumes in the United States and Europe, the effort bombed.

The perfumes—two for women ("Nuit" and "Jour") and two for men ("Bic for Men" and "Bic Sport for Men")—were packaged in quarter-ounce glass spray bottles that looked like fat cigarette lighters and sold for about $5 each. They were displayed in plastic packages on racks at checkout counters throughout Bic's extensive distribution channels, which included 100,000 or so drugstores, supermarkets, and other mass merchandisers. At the time of the launch, a Bic spokesperson described the products as logical extensions of the Bic heritage: "High quality at affordable prices, convenient to purchase and convenient to use." The company spent $20 million on an advertising and promotion blitz that featured images of stylish people enjoying the perfumes and used the tag line "Paris in your pocket."

What went wrong? Although their other products did stand for convenience and for good quality at low prices, Bic's managers didn't understand that the overall brand image lacked a certain cachet with customers—a critical element when marketing something as tied to emotions as perfume. The marketers knew that customers understood the message they were sending with their earlier products. But they didn't have a handle on the associations that the customers had added to the brand image—a utilitarian, impersonal essence—which didn't at all lend itself to perfume.

By contrast, Gillette has been careful not to fall into the Bic trap. While all of its products benefit from a similarly extensive distribution system, it is very protective of the name carried by its razors, blades, and associated toiletries. The company's electric razors, for example, use the entirely separate Braun name, and its oral care products are marketed under the Oral B name.

The brand is given proper support, and that support is sustained over the long run

Brand equity must be carefully constructed. A firm foundation for brand equity requires that consumers have the proper depth and breadth of awareness and strong, favorable, and unique associations with the brand in their memory. Too often, managers want to take shortcuts and bypass more basic branding considerations—such as achieving the necessary level of brand awareness—in favor of concentrating on flashier aspects of brand building related to image.

A good example of lack of support comes from the oil and gas industry in the 1980s. In the late 1970s, consumers had an extremely positive image of Shell Oil and, according to market research, saw clear differences between that brand and its major competitors. In the early 1980s, however, for a variety of reasons, Shell cut back considerably on its advertising and marketing. Shell has yet to regain the ground it lost. The brand no longer enjoys the same special status in the eyes of consumers, who now view it as similar to other oil companies.

Another example is Coors Brewing. As Coors devoted increasing attention to growing the equity of its less-established brands like Coors Light, and introduced new products like Zima, ad support for the flagship beer plummeted from a peak of about $43 million in 1985 to just $4 million in 1993. What's more, the focus of the ads for Coors beer shifted from promoting an iconoclastic, independent, western image to reflecting more contemporary themes. Perhaps not surprisingly, sales of Coors beer dropped by half between 1989 and 1993. Finally in 1994, Coors began to address the problem, launching a campaign to prop up sales that returned to its original focus. Marketers at Coors admit that they did not consistently give the brand the attention it needed. As one commented: "We've not marketed Coors as aggressively as we should have in the past ten to 15 years."

The company monitors sources of brand equity
Strong brands generally make good and frequent use of in-depth brand audits and ongoing brand-tracking studies. A brand audit is an exercise designed to assess the health of a given brand. Typically, it consists of a detailed internal description of exactly how the brand has been marketed (called a "brand inventory") and a thorough external investigation, through focus groups and other consumer research, of exactly what the brand does and could mean to consumers (called a "brand exploratory"). Brand audits are particularly useful when they are scheduled on a periodic basis. It's critical for managers holding the reins of a brand portfolio to get a clear picture of the products and services being offered and how they are being marketed and branded. It's also important to see how that same picture looks to customers. Tapping customers' perceptions and beliefs

often uncovers the true meaning of a brand, or group of brands, revealing where corporate and consumer views conflict and thus showing managers exactly where they have to refine or redirect their branding efforts or their marketing goals.

Tracking studies can build on brand audits by employing quantitative measures to provide current information about how a brand is performing for any given dimension. Generally, a tracking study will collect information on consumers' perceptions, attitudes, and behaviors on a routine basis over time; a thorough study can yield valuable tactical insights into the short-term effectiveness of marketing programs and activities. Whereas brand audits measure where the brand has been, tracking studies measure where the brand is now and whether marketing programs are having their intended effects.

The strongest brands, however, are also supported by formal brand-equity-management systems. Managers of these brands have a written document—a "brand equity charter"—that spells out the company's general philosophy with respect to brands and brand equity as concepts (what a brand is, why brands matter, why brand management is relevant to the company, and so on). It also summarizes the activities that make up brand audits, brand tracking, and other brand research; specifies the outcomes expected of them; and includes the latest findings gathered from such research. The charter then lays out guidelines for implementing brand strategies and tactics and documents proper treatment of the brand's trademark—the rules for how the logo can appear and be used on packaging, in ads, and so forth. These managers also assemble the results of their various tracking surveys and other relevant measures into a brand equity report, which is distributed to management on a monthly, quarterly, or annual basis. The brand equity report not only describes what is happening within a brand but also why.

Even a market leader can benefit by carefully monitoring its brand, as Disney aptly demonstrates. In the late 1980s, Disney became concerned that some of its characters (among them Mickey Mouse and Donald Duck) were being used inappropriately and becoming overexposed. To determine the severity of the problem, Disney undertook an extensive brand audit. First, as part of the brand inventory, managers compiled a list of all available Disney products (manufactured by the company and licensed) and all third-party promotions (complete with point-of-purchase displays and relevant merchandising) in stores worldwide. At the same time, as part of a brand exploratory, Disney launched its first major consumer research study to investigate how consumers felt about the Disney brand.

The results of the brand inventory were a revelation to senior managers. The Disney characters were on so many products and marketed in so many ways that it was difficult to understand how or why many of the decisions had been made in the first place. The consumer study only reinforced their concerns. The study indicated that people lumped all the product endorsements together. Disney was Disney to consumers, whether they saw the characters in films, or heard them in recordings, or associated them with theme parks or products.

Consequently, all products and services that used the Disney name or characters had an impact on Disney's brand equity. And because of the characters' broad exposure in the marketplace, many consumers had begun to feel that Disney was exploiting its name. Disney characters were used in a promotion of Johnson Wax, for instance, a product that would seemingly leverage almost nothing of value from the Disney name. Consumers were even upset when Disney characters were linked to well-regarded premium brands like Tide laundry detergent. In that case, consumers felt the characters added little value to the product. Worse yet, they were annoyed that the characters involved children in a purchasing decision that they otherwise would probably have ignored.

If consumers reacted so negatively to associating Disney with a strong brand like Tide, imagine how they reacted when they saw the hundreds of other Disney-licensed products and joint promotions. Disney's characters were hawking everything from diapers to cars to McDonald's hamburgers. Consumers reported that they resented all the endorsements because they felt they had a special, personal relationship with the characters and with Disney that should not be handled so carelessly.

As a result of the brand inventory and exploratory, Disney moved quickly to establish a brand equity team to better manage the brand franchise and more selectively evaluate licensing and other third-party promotional opportunities. One of the mandates of this team was to ensure that a consistent image for Disney—reinforcing its key association with fun family entertainment—was conveyed by all third-party products and services. Subsequently, Disney declined an offer to cobrand a mutual fund designed to help parents save for their children's college expenses. Although there was a family association, managers felt that a connection with the financial community suggested associations that were inconsistent with other aspects of the brand's image.

The Value of Balance

Building a strong brand involves maximizing all ten characteristics. And that is, clearly, a worthy goal. But in practice, it is tremendously difficult because in many cases when a company focuses on improving one, others may suffer.

Consider a premium brand facing a new market entrant with comparable features at a lower price. The brand's managers might be tempted to rethink their pricing strategy. Lowering prices might successfully block the new entrant from gaining market share in the short term. But what effect would that have in the long term? Will stepping outside its definition of "premium" change the brand in the minds of its target customers? Will it create the impression that the brand is no longer top of the line or that the innovation is no longer solid? Will the brand's message become cloudy? The price change may in fact attract customers from a different market segment to try the brand, producing a short-term blip in sales. But will those customers be the true target? Will their purchases put off the brand's original market?

The trick is to get a handle on how a brand performs on all ten attributes and then to evaluate any move from all possible perspectives. How will this new ad campaign affect customers' perception of price? How will this new product line affect the brand hierarchy in our portfolio? Does this tweak in positioning gain enough ground to offset any potential damage caused if customers feel we've been inconsistent?

One would think that monitoring brand performance wouldn't necessarily be included in the equation. But even effectively monitoring brand performance can have negative repercussions if you just go through the motions or don't follow through decisively on what you've learned.

Levi-Strauss's experiences are telling. In the mid-1990s, the company put together a comprehensive brand-equity-measurement system. Practically from the time the system was installed, it indicated that the brand image was beginning to slip, both in terms of the appeal of Levi's tight-fitting flagship 501 brand of jeans and how contemporary and cutting edge the overall Levi's brand was. The youth market was going for a much baggier look; competitors were rushing in to fill the gap. Distracted in part by an internal reengineering effort, however, Levi's was slow to respond and when it did, it came up with underfunded, transparently trendy ad campaigns that failed to resonate with its young target market. Its market share in the jeans category plummeted in the latter half of the 1990s. The result? Levi's has terminated its decades-long relationship with ad agency Foote, Cone & Belding and is now attempting to launch new products and new ad campaigns. For Levi's, putting in the system was not enough; perhaps if it had adhered more closely to other branding principles, concentrating on innovating and staying relevant to its customers, it could have better leveraged its market research data.

Negative examples and cautionary words abound, of course. But it is important to recognize that in strong brands the top ten traits have a positive, synergistic effect on one another; excelling at one characteristic makes it easier to excel at another. A deep understanding of a brand's meaning and a well-defined brand position, for example, guide development of an optimal marketing program. That, in turn, might lead to a more appropriate value-pricing strategy. Similarly, instituting an effective brand-equity-measurement system can help clarify a brand's meaning, capture consumers' reactions to pricing changes and other strategic shifts, and monitor the brand's ability to stay relevant to consumers through innovation.

Brand Equity as a Bridge

Ultimately, the power of a brand lies in the minds of consumers or customers, in what they have experienced and learned about the brand over time. Consumer knowledge is really at the heart of brand equity. This realization has important managerial implications.

In an abstract sense, brand equity provides marketers with a strategic bridge from their past to their future. That is, all the dollars spent each year on marketing can be thought of not so much as expenses but as investments—investments in what consumers know, feel, recall, believe, and think about the brand. And that knowledge dictates appropriate and inappropriate future directions for the brand—for it is consumers who will decide, based on their beliefs and attitudes about a given brand, where they think that brand should go and grant permission (or not) to any marketing tactic or program. If not properly designed and implemented, those expenditures may not be good investments—the right knowledge structures may not have been created in consumers' minds—but they are investments nonetheless.

Ultimately, the value to marketers of brand equity as a concept depends on how they use it. Brand equity can help marketers focus, giving them a way to interpret their past marketing performance and design their future marketing programs. Everything the company does can help enhance or detract from brand equity. Marketers who build strong brands have embraced the concept and use it to its fullest to clarify, implement, and communicate their marketing strategy.

KEVIN LANE KELLER is the E.B. Osborn Professor of Marketing at the Tuck School of Business at Dartmouth College.

Originally published in January 2000. Reprint R00104

The Female Economy

by Michael J. Silverstein and Kate Sayre

WOMEN NOW DRIVE THE WORLD economy. Globally, they control about $20 trillion in annual consumer spending, and that figure could climb as high as $28 trillion in the next five years. Their $13 trillion in total yearly earnings could reach $18 trillion in the same period. In aggregate, women represent a growth market bigger than China and India combined—more than twice as big, in fact. Given those numbers, it would be foolish to ignore or underestimate the female consumer. And yet many companies do just that, even ones that are confident they have a winning strategy when it comes to women.

Consider Dell's short-lived effort to market laptops specifically to women. The company fell into the classic "make it pink" mind-set with the May 2009 launch of its Della website. The site emphasized colors, computer accessories, and tips for counting calories and finding recipes. It created an uproar among women, who described it as "slick but disconcerting" and "condescending."

The blogosphere reacted quickly to the company's "very special site for women." Austin Modine of the online tech publication *The Register* responded acidly, "If you thought computer shopping was a gender-neutral affair, then you've obviously been struck down by an acute case of female hysteria. (Nine out of ten Victorian-age doctors agree.)" The *New York Times* said that Dell had to go to the "school of marketing hard knocks." Within weeks of the launch, the company altered the site's name and focus. "You spoke, we listened," Dell told users. Kudos to Dell for correcting course promptly, but why didn't its marketers catch the potentially awkward positioning before the launch?

Most companies have much to learn about selling to women. In 2008 the Boston Consulting Group fielded a comprehensive study of how women felt about their work and their lives, and how they were being served by businesses. It turned out there was lots of room for improvement. More than 12,000 women, from more than 40 geographies and a variety of income levels and walks of life, responded to our survey. They answered—often with disarming candor—120 questions about their education and finances, homes and possessions, jobs and careers, activities and interests, relationships, and hopes and fears, along with their shopping behavior and spending patterns in some three dozen categories of goods and services. (You can learn more about the survey and take an abridged version of it at www.womenspeakworldwide.com.) We also conducted hundreds of interviews and studied women working in 50 organizations in 13 fields of endeavor.

Idea in Brief

As a market, women represent an opportunity bigger than China and India combined. They control $20 trillion in consumer spending, and that figure could reach $28 trillion in the next five years. Women drive the world economy, in fact. Yet most companies do a remarkably poor job of serving them, a new study by the Boston Consulting Group reveals. BCG surveyed more than 12,000 women from a variety of geographies, income levels, and walks of life about their education, finances, homes, jobs, activities, interests, relationships, hopes, and fears, as well as their shopping behaviors and spending patterns. In this article, Silverstein and Sayre, two of the firm's partners, review highlights of the findings and explain the biggest opportunities. While any business would be wise to target female consumers, they say, the greatest potential lies in six industries: food, fitness, beauty, apparel, health care, and financial services. Address women's concerns effectively, and your company could see the kind of rapid growth that fitness chain Curves enjoyed. Most health clubs are expensive and designed for men, with lots of complicated bodybuilding equipment. Curves, however, understood that time-pressed women needed quick, affordable workouts, and came up with the concept of simple, 30-minute exercise routines geared to women and offered in no-frills spaces. Companies that likewise successfully tailor their offerings to women will be positioned to win when the economy begins to recover.

Here's what we found, in brief: Women feel vastly underserved. Despite the remarkable strides in market power and social position that they have made in the past century, they still appear to be undervalued in the marketplace and underestimated in the workplace. They have too many demands on their time and constantly juggle conflicting priorities—work, home, and family. Few companies have responded to their need for time-saving solutions or for products and services designed specifically for them.

The world's largest opportunity

A growth forecast (in trillions)

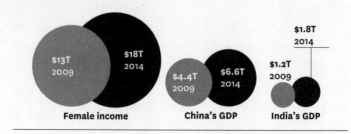

It's still tough for women to find a pair of pants, buy a healthful meal, get financial advice without feeling patronized, or make the time to stay in shape. Although women control spending in most categories of consumer goods, too many businesses behave as if they had no say over purchasing decisions. Companies continue to offer them poorly conceived products and services and outdated marketing narratives that promote female stereotypes. Look at the automotive industry. Cars are designed for speed—not utility, which is what really matters to women. No SUV is built to accommodate a mother who needs to load two small children into it. Or consider a recent ad for Bounty paper towels, in which a husband and son stand by watching a spill cross the room, until Mom comes along and cheerfully cleans up the mess.

Meanwhile, women are increasingly gaining influence in the work world. As we write, the number of working women in the United States is about to surpass the number of working men. Three-quarters of the people who have lost jobs in the current recession are men. To be fair, women are still paid less, on average, than men, and are more likely to work part-time—factors that have helped insulate them somewhat from the crisis. Nevertheless, we believe that as this recession abates, women not only will represent one of the largest market opportunities in our lifetimes but also will be an important force in spurring a recovery and generating new prosperity.

Where the Opportunities Lie

Each person's story is different, but when we looked for patterns in our findings, we identified six basic archetypes among our respondents. These types, which are primarily defined by income, age, and stage of life, are *fast-tracker, pressure cooker, relationship focused, managing on her own, fulfilled empty nester,* and *making ends meet*. Few women fall into just one type. Married fast-trackers with children, for instance, are likely at some point in their lives to also fall into the pressure cooker category. (See the exhibit "Six key female consumer segments.")

Despite its limitations, such segmentation is useful in informing the development and marketing of companies' offerings. Knowing whom you're targeting and what she looks for in the marketplace can be a tremendous source of advantage.

Any company would be wise to target female customers, but the greatest potential lies in six industries. Four are businesses where women are most likely to

Six key female consumer segments

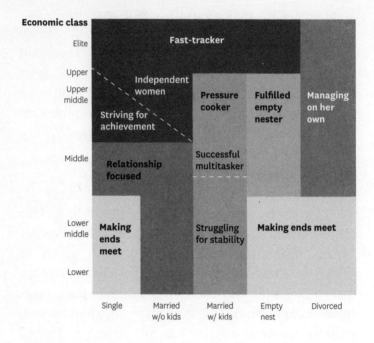

spend more or trade up: food, fitness, beauty, and apparel. The other two are businesses with which women have made their dissatisfaction very clear: financial services and health care.

Food represents one of the largest opportunities. Women are responsible for the lion's share of grocery shopping and meal preparation. Food is also one of consumers' most important budget items, one that can be adjusted but never eliminated.

Fast-tracker
24% of population
34% of earned income
- Economic and educational elite
- Seeks adventure and learning

Subsegments:
- Striving for achievement – 15% of population, 19% of earned income; job and recognition are priorities
- Independent women – 9% of population, 15% of earned income; works the most; prizes autonomy

Pressure cooker
22% of population
23% of earned income
- Married with children
- Feels ignored and stereotyped

Subsegments:
- Successful multitasker – 10% of population, 14% of earned income; feels in control
- Struggling for stability – 12% of population, 9% of earned income; constantly battles chaos

Relationship focused
16% of population
13% of earned income
- Content and optimistic
- Isn't pressed for time
- Has ample discretionary income
- Focuses on experiences, not products

Managing on her own
10% of population
9% of earned income
- Single again – divorced or widowed
- Seeks ways to form connections

Fulfilled empty nester
15% of population
16% of earned income
- Largely ignored by marketers
- Concerned about health and aging gracefully
- Focused on travel, exercise, and leisure

Making ends meet
12% of population
5% of earned income
- No money for beauty or exercise
- Majority lack college education
- Seeks credit, value, and small luxuries

Favorite grocery stores among the women we surveyed included Whole Foods and Tesco. Though they appeal to different segments, the two chains have each developed a loyal following. Whole Foods has succeeded despite its high prices by targeting the demanding (but well-to-do) fast-trackers, who want high-quality meats and produce and a knowledgeable staff. Tesco stores, which offer one-stop shopping for a wide range of household items, including books, furniture, and financial services, appeal to the time-strapped pressure cookers, who desire convenience.

Fitness is also a big business. In the United States alone the market for diet food has been growing 6% to 9% a year and is worth approximately $10 billion, while the worldwide market is worth about $20 billion. The U.S. health club industry generates revenues of about $14 billion annually.

About two-thirds of our survey respondents described themselves as overweight; what was until recently an American issue has become a global phenomenon. But while women say that their fitness is a priority, in reality it tends to take a backseat. When asked to prioritize the needs of spouses, children, parents, and themselves, nearly all women ranked their own needs second or third—which means they have trouble finding time to work out.

The challenge for companies is to make fitness more accessible to women. For instance, most health clubs are expensive and designed for men. They can feel more like nightclubs than fitness centers and are geared to bodybuilders. Generally, women are less interested in pumping themselves up than in shedding a few pounds, improving their cardiovascular health, and getting toned. Bright lights, electronic music, sweaty men, and complicated equipment are often a turnoff.

The fitness chain Curves recognized and responded to women's concerns—and grew quickly as a result. Curves has a very simple concept: cheap, fast exercise for women only, with no-frills spaces suited to middle-aged clients of average build. Helpers stand by to usher them through a simple 30-minute circuit, so there's no need to hire a trainer.

Beauty products and services promote a sense of emotional well-being in women. Those we talked with who spent a higher portion of their income on cosmetics felt more satisfied, successful, and powerful; they also reported lower levels of stress even if they worked longer hours.

But even so, women are fundamentally dissatisfied with beauty offerings, and the way the industry is evolving keeps them from spending as much as they might. For one thing, there are too many choices; it's a male-dominated industry in which men make hit-or-miss guesses about what women want, and products come and go at a rapid pace. Women are passionate about the industry and well represented in jobs at the entry level, but female employment drops off at the executive and senior leadership levels. A good first step toward gaining market share might be to put more women at the top—where they can help make key decisions and provide input about what does and doesn't resonate with customers.

Many companies that do well in beauty have made creative use of new technologies to address women's desire to look younger. Facial skin-care products, for instance, have grown into a $20 billion category worldwide. Whereas shelves used to be lined with products whose sole purpose was to moisturize the skin, now there are formulas containing a variety of benefits, such as sun protection, skin plumping, and capillary strengthening—all designed to prevent, or at the very least disguise, aging.

At the top of the range is Switzerland-based La Prairie's Cellular Cream Platinum Rare antiaging moisturizer, which goes for $1,000 for 1.7 ounces. The cream contains a trace of platinum, which, the company claims, "recharges the skin's electrical balance and protects the skin's DNA." Despite the price, customers lined up at luxury retail stores to purchase a jar when the cream was introduced in 2008.

At the other end of the range, Procter & Gamble's Olay brand is available in drugstores. It has morphed from one low-end product with a simple purpose (moisturizing), which about 2% of the population used, into an array of higher-end products with numerous applications and a 40% household penetration. One of the most successful new Olay products is its Regenerist Daily Regenerating Serum, advertised as the next-best thing to cosmetic surgery.

Apparel—including accessories and shoes—is a $47 billion global industry with plenty of room for improvement, primarily when it comes to fit and affordability.

Most women are not a perfect size 6, and they don't like to be reminded of it every time they shop. Trying on clothes is often an exercise in frustration that just reinforces women's negative body images. Banana Republic, a favorite retailer of the women in our survey, has won a loyal following by taking steps to solve the problem of fit, particularly for pants. It offers a variety of cuts to suit different figures, and sizes are consistent across the board. Once you discover your "fit block" (the chain's technical term for body type), you can buy multiple pairs of pants, even online, quickly and

Women control the lion's share of consumer spending

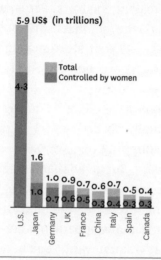

dependably. Banana Republic has become Gap's most profitable brand, the only one that's grown over the past five years.

By contrast, Express stores focused on style and color but failed to deliver a consistent fit. Women might try on four garments marked "size 8" that actually varied in size from 6 to 12. The chain's sales began to lag so much that its parent company, Limited Brands, ended up exiting the fashion apparel business; it sold Express to a private equity group in 2007.

The costliness of clothing was another sore point for the women in our survey. That explains why respondents also favored Sweden-based H&M. Its stores offer inexpensive, fun, trendy clothes and, with a rapid turnover of stock, an element of surprise each time shoppers visit. Women value the ability to buy a new outfit without breaking the bank. Perhaps contributing to H&M's success is the fact that nearly 80% of the company's employees, 77% of store managers, and 44% of country managers are women. So are seven of the 11 board members.

Few of the women we talked to during the course of our research actually needed new clothing. Most could get away with shopping once or twice a year just to replenish the basics. But given that women say they are willing to spend extra to find clothing that really works for them, manufacturers and retailers can find plenty of untapped potential in the apparel market—if they listen carefully to what women want, seek new technologies that offer superior fabrication and color, and improve comfort and fit.

Financial services wins the prize as the industry least sympathetic to women—and one in which companies stand to gain the most if they can change their approach.

Despite setbacks in the economy, private wealth in the United States is expected to grow from some $14 trillion today to $22 trillion by 2020, and 50% of it will be in the hands of women. Yet women are still continually let down by the level of quality and service they get from financial companies, which presume men to be their target customers.

Our survey respondents were scathing in their comments about financial institutions. They cited a lack of respect, poor advice, contradictory policies, one-size-fits-all forms, and a seemingly endless tangle of red tape that leaves them exhausted and annoyed. Consider just a few quotations from our interviews:

- "I hate being stereotyped because of my gender and age, and I don't appreciate being treated like an infant."
- "As a single woman, I often feel that financial services institutions aren't looking for my business."
- "Financial service reps talk down to women as if we cannot understand more than just the basics."
- "I'm earning close to $1 million a year and should retire with $20 million plus in assets, so I'm not right for a cookie cutter discount broker, nor qualified for high-end wealth management services."

An unhappy customer with $20 million plus to invest represents a golden opportunity. Overall, the markets for investment services and life insurance for women are wide open. (For three of the largest opportunities, see the exhibit "Financial categories where untapped sales to women are worth trillions.")

Health care was a source of frustration for women in our survey—and for middle-aged respondents in particular. Women resoundingly reported dissatisfaction with their hospitals and doctors. When polled about the service provided by their general practitioners and specialists, more than 60% of them said those doctors could do "somewhat better" or "significantly better." Seventy-one percent of women aged 30 to 49 were

Financial categories where untapped sales to women are worth trillions

Extraordinary amounts of money are up for grabs in the financial services business. The most lucrative opportunities for companies arise at transition points like marriage, divorce, childbirth, and a job change, because women are most likely to make investment decisions around such events.

	Investments & financial advisory	Life insurance	Payments
Unmet needs	• Financial education • Advisers that understand and cater to female life events • Equal treatment with men	• Education about insuring entire household versus just the primary earner • Equitable coverage for working women and men • Valuations for "at-home" work	• Reward programs and payment plans that cater to women
Potential value in U.S.	• About $2.1 trillion in wealth held by high-net-worth divorced or widowed women	• About $2 trillion in incremental coverage	• About $1.4 trillion in credit card purchases
Goals	• Win market share • Grow market	• Grow market • Create new market	• Win market share • Grow market
Key inflection points to target	• Divorce • Death of a spouse	• Marriage • First home purchase • Promotion • Birth of first child	• First credit card • College commencement • First job

dissatisfied with general practitioners, and 68% of that group were dissatisfied with specialists. More specifically, they were irritated by the amount of time they spent waiting for doctors and lab results, and scheduling and keeping appointments for themselves and their families. Making matters worse, women generally pay significantly more than men do for health insurance.

Again, the opportunities for companies that do cater to women are enormous. Johnson & Johnson, though not a health care services provider, was almost invariably represented (in the form of oral contraception, baby care, bandages, and other products) when we peeked into our respondents' medicine cabinets. The company spends 4% of its sales on consumer research and development—more than twice the industry average—and thus in all likelihood has a better understanding of its female customers than most companies in its space do. For instance, because mothers of young children are one of its important customer groups, the company conducted a clinical study in partnership with a pediatric sleep expert at the Children's Hospital of Philadelphia. Together, they developed a three-step routine to help babies sleep better, consisting of bath, massage, and quiet time. J&J then launched a line of products to complement the routine—with the results of the clinical study to boost their credibility.

Overburdened and Overwhelmed

Considering how often the issue of time—and not enough of it—came up in our survey and our interviews, offering easier and more convenient ways to make purchases would create a clear advantage in all the industries we've discussed. We've seen that women don't make enough time for themselves. They are still far more burdened than men by household tasks;

according to our survey, about one-third of men don't help their spouse or partner with chores. In Japan women receive the least support, with 74% getting little or no help from their spouses. At the opposite extreme, 71% of Indian husbands pitch in on household chores.

Our research also showed that pressures change over time. Women are happiest in their early and later years and experience their lowest point in their early and mid forties. That's when they face the greatest challenges in managing work and home, and must deal with caring for both children and aging parents. So this group is especially receptive to products and services that can help them better control their lives and balance their priorities.

A Future of Parity, Power, and Influence

When the dust from the economic crisis settles, we predict, women will occupy an even more important position in the economy and the world order than they now do. What might that economy look like? In some ways it will be characterized by the same trends we've seen over the past five decades. For one thing, women will represent an ever-larger proportion of the workforce. The number of working women has been increasing by about 2.2% a year. We expect an additional 90 million or so women to enter the workforce by 2013, perhaps even more as employment becomes a necessity. At nearly every major consumer company, most middle managers are women. It's only a matter of time before they rise to more-senior positions. Already, women own

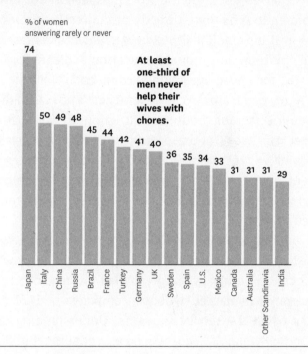

How often does your spouse or partner help with household chores?

% of women answering rarely or never

At least one-third of men never help their wives with chores.

Japan 74, Italy 50, China 49, Russia 48, Brazil 45, France 44, Turkey 42, Germany 41, UK 40, Sweden 36, Spain 35, U.S. 34, Mexico 33, Canada 31, Australia 31, Other Scandinavia 31, India 29

40% of the businesses in the United States, and their businesses are growing at twice the rate of U.S. firms as a whole. (Admittedly, the numbers are being skewed as small businesses position themselves for government contracts that favor female-owned companies.) Women will also continue to struggle with work/life balance, conflicting demands, and too little time.

Once companies wake up to the potential of the female economy, they will find a whole new range of commercial opportunities in women's social concerns. Women seek to buy products and services from companies that do good for the world, especially for other women. Brands that—directly or indirectly—promote physical and emotional well-being, protect and preserve the environment, provide education and care for the needy, and encourage love and connection will benefit.

And women are the customer. There's no reason they should settle for products that ignore or fail to fully meet their needs, or that do so cynically or superficially. Women will increasingly resist being stereotyped, segmented only by age or income, lumped together into an "all women" characterization, or, worse, undifferentiated from men.

The financial crisis will come to an end, and now is the time to lay the foundation for postrecession growth. A focus on women as a target market—instead of on any geographical market—will up a company's odds of success when the recovery begins. Understanding and meeting women's needs will be essential to rebuilding the economy; therein lies the key to breakout growth, loyalty, and market share.

MICHAEL J. SILVERSTEIN is a senior partner in the Boston Consulting Group's Chicago office. **KATE SAYRE** is a partner in BCG's New York office.

Originally published in September 2009. Reprint R0909D

Customer Value Propositions in Business Markets

by James C. Anderson, James A. Narus, and Wouter van Rossum

"CUSTOMER VALUE PROPOSITION" has become one of the most widely used terms in business markets in recent years. Yet our management-practice research reveals that there is no agreement as to what constitutes a customer value proposition—or what makes one persuasive. Moreover, we find that most value propositions make claims of savings and benefits to the customer without backing them up. An offering may actually provide superior value—but if the supplier doesn't demonstrate and document that claim, a customer manager will likely dismiss it as marketing puffery. Customer managers, increasingly held accountable for reducing costs, don't have the luxury of simply believing suppliers' assertions.

Take the case of a company that makes integrated circuits (ICs). It hoped to supply 5 million units to an electronic device manufacturer for its next-generation product. In the course of negotiations, the supplier's salesperson learned that he was competing against a company whose price was 10 cents lower per unit. The customer asked each salesperson why his company's offering was superior. This salesperson based his value proposition on the service that he, personally, would provide.

Unbeknownst to the salesperson, the customer had built a customer value model, which found that the company's offering, though 10 cents higher in price per IC, was actually worth 15.9 cents more. The electronics engineer who was leading the development project had recommended that the purchasing manager buy those ICs, even at the higher price. The service was, indeed, worth something in the model—but just 0.2 cents! Unfortunately, the salesperson had overlooked the two elements of his company's IC offering that were most valuable to the customer, evidently unaware how much they were worth to that customer and, objectively, how superior they made his company's offering to that of the competitor. Not surprisingly, when push came to shove, perhaps suspecting that his service was not worth the difference in price, the salesperson offered a 10-cent price concession to win the business—consequently leaving at least a half million dollars on the table.

Some managers view the customer value proposition as a form of spin their marketing departments develop for advertising and promotional copy. This shortsighted view neglects the very real contribution of value propositions to superior business performance. Properly

Idea in Brief

If you sell products to other companies, you know how hard it's become to win their business. Your customers—pressured to control costs—seem to care only about price. But if you lower prices to stimulate sales, your profits shrink.

So how *can* you persuade your business customers to pay the premium prices your offerings deserve? Craft a compelling **customer value proposition**. Research potential customers' enterprises, identifying their unique requirements. Then explain how your offerings outmatch your rivals' on the criteria that matter *most* to customers. Document the cost savings and profits your products deliver to existing customers—and will deliver to new customers.

The payoff? You help your customers slash costs—while generating profitable growth for yourself. One company that manufactured resins used in exterior paints discovered this firsthand. By researching the needs of commercial painting contractors—a key customer segment—the company learned that labor constituted the lion's share of contractors' costs, while paint made up just 15% of costs. Armed with this insight, the resin maker emphasized that its product dried so fast that contractors could apply two coats in one day—substantially lowering labor costs. Customers snapped up the product—and happily shelled out a 40% price premium for it.

constructed, they force companies to rigorously focus on what their offerings are really worth to their customers. Once companies become disciplined about understanding customers, they can make smarter choices about where to allocate scarce company resources in developing new offerings.

We conducted management-practice research over the past two years in Europe and the United States to understand what constitutes a customer value proposition

Idea in Practice

To craft compelling customer value propositions:

Understand Customers' Businesses

Invest time and effort to understand your customers' businesses and identify their unique requirements and preferences.

Example: The resin manufacturer deepened its understanding of key customers in several ways. It enrolled managers in courses on how painting contractors estimate jobs. It conducted focus groups and field tests to study products' performance on crucial criteria. It also asked customers to identify performance trade-offs they were willing to make and to indicate their willingness to pay for paints that delivered enhanced performance. And it stayed current on customer needs by joining industry associations composed of key customer segments.

Substantiate Your Value Claims

"We can save you money!" won't cut it as a customer value proposition. Back up this claim in accessible, persuasive language that describes the differences between your offerings and rivals'. And explain how those differences translate into monetary worth for customers.

Example: Rockwell Automation precisely calculated cost savings from reduced power usage that customers would gain by purchasing Rockwell's pump solution instead of a competitor's comparable offering. Rockwell used industry-specific metrics to communicate about functionality and

and what makes one persuasive to customers. One striking discovery is that it is exceptionally difficult to find examples of value propositions that resonate with customers. Here, drawing on the best practices of a handful of suppliers in business markets, we present a systematic approach for developing value propositions that are meaningful to target customers and that focus suppliers' efforts on creating superior value.

performance—including kilowatt-hours spent, number of operating hours per year, and dollars per kilowatt-hour.

Document Value Delivered

Create written accounts of cost savings or added value that existing customers have actually captured by using your offerings. And conduct on-site pilots at prospective customer locations to gather data on your products' performance.

Example: Chemical manufacturer Akzo Nobel conducted a two-week pilot on a production reactor at a prospective customer's facility. AN's goal? To study the performance of its high-purity metal organics product relative to the next best alternative in producing compound semiconductor wafers. The study proved that AN's product was as good as or better than rivals' *and* that it significantly lowered energy and maintenance costs.

Make Customer Value Proposition a Central Business Skill

Improve and reward managers' ability to craft compelling customer value propositions.

Example: Quaker Chemical conducts a value-proposition training program annually for chemical program managers. The managers review case studies from industries Quaker serves and participate in simulated customer interviews to gather information needed to devise proposals. The team with the best proposal earns "bragging rights"— highly valued in Quaker's competitive culture. Managers who develop proposals that their director deems viable win gift certificates.

Three Kinds of Value Propositions

We have classified the ways that suppliers use the term "value proposition" into three types: all benefits, favorable points of difference, and resonating focus. (See the exhibit "Which alternative conveys value to customers?")

Which alternative conveys value to customers?

Suppliers use the term "value proposition" three different ways. Most managers simply list all the benefits they believe that their offering might deliver to target customers. The more they can think of, the better. Some managers do recognize that the customer has an alternative, but they often make the mistake of assuming that favorable points of difference must be valuable for the customer. Best-practice suppliers base their value proposition on the few elements that matter most to target customers, demonstrate the value of this superior performance, and communicate it in a way that conveys a sophisticated understanding of the customer's business priorities.

Value proposition:	All benefits	Favorable points of difference	Resonating focus
Consists of:	All benefits customers receive from a market offering	All favorable points of difference a market offering has relative to the next best alternative	The one or two points of difference (and, perhaps, a point of parity) whose improvement will deliver the greatest value to the customer for the foreseeable future
Answers the customer question:	"Why should our firm purchase your offering?"	"Why should our firm purchase your offering instead of your competitor's?"	"What is most worthwhile for our firm to keep in mind about your offering?"
Requires:	Knowledge of own market offering	Knowledge of own market offering and next best alternative	Knowledge of how own market offering delivers superior value to customers, compared with next best alternative
Has the potential pitfall:	Benefit assertion	Value presumption	Requires customer value research

All Benefits

Our research indicates that most managers, when asked to construct a customer value proposition, simply list all the benefits they believe that their offering might deliver to target customers. The more they can think of, the better. This approach requires the least knowledge about customers and competitors and, thus, the least amount of work to construct. However, its relative simplicity has a major potential drawback: *benefit assertion*. Managers may claim advantages for features that actually provide no benefit to target customers.

Such was the case with a company that sold high-performance gas chromatographs to R&D laboratories in large companies, universities, and government agencies in the Benelux countries. One feature of a particular chromatograph allowed R&D lab customers to maintain a high degree of sample integrity. Seeking growth, the company began to market the most basic model of this chromatograph to a new segment: commercial laboratories. In initial meetings with prospective customers, the firm's salespeople touted the benefits of maintaining sample integrity. Their prospects scoffed at this benefit assertion, stating that they routinely tested soil and water samples, for which maintaining sample integrity was not a concern. The supplier was taken aback and forced to rethink its value proposition.

Another pitfall of the all benefits value proposition is that many, even most, of the benefits may be points of parity with those of the next best alternative, diluting the effect of the few genuine points of difference. Managers need to clearly identify in their customer value

> ## The Building Blocks of a Successful Customer Value Proposition
>
> **A SUPPLIER'S OFFERING MAY HAVE** many technical, economic, service, or social benefits that deliver value to customers—but in all probability, so do competitors' offerings. Thus, the essential question is, "How do these value elements compare with those of the next best alternative?" We've found that it's useful to sort value elements into three types.
>
> *Points of parity* are elements with essentially the same performance or functionality as those of the next best alternative.
>
> *Points of difference* are elements that make the supplier's offering either superior or inferior to the next best alternative.
>
> *Points of contention* are elements about which the supplier and its customers disagree regarding how their performance or functionality compares with those of the next best alternative. Either the supplier regards a value element as a point of difference in its favor, while the customer regards that element as a point of parity with the next best alternative, or the supplier regards a value element as a point of parity, while the customer regards it as a point of difference in favor of the next best alternative.

propositions which elements are points of parity and which are points of difference. (See the sidebar "The Building Blocks of a Successful Customer Value Proposition.") For example, an international engineering consultancy was bidding for a light-rail project. The last chart of the company's presentation listed ten reasons why the municipality should award the project to the firm. But the chart had little persuasive power because the other two finalists could make most of the same claims.

Put yourself, for a moment, in the place of the prospective client. Suppose each firm, at the end of its presentation, gives ten reasons why you ought to award it the project, and the lists from all the firms are almost the same. If each firm is saying essentially the same thing, how do you make a choice? You ask each of the firms to give a final, best price, and then you award the project to the firm that gives the largest price concession. Any distinctions that do exist have been overshadowed by the firms' greater sameness.

Favorable Points of Difference
The second type of value proposition explicitly recognizes that the customer has an alternative. The recent experience of a leading industrial gas supplier illustrates this perspective. A customer sent the company a request for proposal stating that the two or three suppliers that could demonstrate the most persuasive value propositions would be invited to visit the customer to discuss and refine their proposals. After this meeting, the customer would select a sole supplier for this business. As this example shows, "Why should our firm purchase your offering instead of your competitor's?" is a more pertinent question than "Why should our firm purchase your offering?" The first question focuses suppliers on differentiating their offerings from the next best alternative, a process that requires detailed knowledge of that alternative, whether it be buying a competitor's offering or solving the customer's problem in a different way.

Knowing that an element of an offering is a point of difference relative to the next best alternative does not, however, convey the value of this difference to target customers. Furthermore, a product or service may have several points of difference, complicating the supplier's understanding of which ones deliver the greatest value. Without a detailed understanding of the customer's requirements and preferences, and what it is worth to fulfill them, suppliers may stress points of difference that deliver relatively little value to the target customer. Each of these can lead to the pitfall of *value presumption:* assuming that favorable points of difference must be valuable for the customer. Our opening anecdote about the IC supplier that unnecessarily discounted its price exemplifies this pitfall.

Resonating Focus

Although the favorable points of difference value proposition is preferable to an all benefits proposition for companies crafting a consumer value proposition, the resonating focus value proposition should be the gold standard. This approach acknowledges that the managers who make purchase decisions have major, ever-increasing levels of responsibility and often are pressed for time. They want to do business with suppliers that fully grasp critical issues in their business and deliver a customer value proposition that's simple yet powerfully captivating. Suppliers can provide such a customer value proposition by making their offerings superior on the few elements that matter most to target customers, demonstrating and documenting the value of this superior performance, and communicating it in a way that conveys a sophisticated understanding of the customer's business priorities.

This type of proposition differs from favorable points of difference in two significant respects. First, more is not better. Although a supplier's offering may possess several favorable points of difference, the resonating focus proposition steadfastly concentrates on the one or two points of difference that deliver, and whose improvement will continue to deliver, the greatest value to target customers. To better leverage limited resources, a supplier might even cede to the next best alternative the favorable points of difference that customers value least, so that the supplier can concentrate its resources on improving the one or two points of difference customers value most. Second, the resonating focus proposition may contain a point of parity. This occurs either when the point of parity is required for target customers even to consider the supplier's offering or when a supplier wants to counter customers' mistaken perceptions that a particular value element is a point of difference in favor of a competitor's offering. This latter case arises when customers believe that the competitor's offering is superior but the supplier believes its offerings are comparable—customer value research provides empirical support for the supplier's assertion.

To give practical meaning to resonating focus, consider the following example. Sonoco, a global packaging supplier headquartered in Hartsville, South Carolina, approached a large European customer, a maker of consumer packaged goods, about redesigning the packaging for one of its product lines. Sonoco believed that the customer would profit from updated packaging, and, by proposing the initiative itself, Sonoco reinforced its reputation as an innovator. Although the redesigned packaging provided six favorable points of difference relative to the next best alternative, Sonoco chose to emphasize one point of parity and two points of difference in what it called its distinctive value proposition (DVP). The value proposition was that the redesigned packaging would deliver significantly greater manufacturing efficiency in the customer's fill lines, through higher-speed closing, and provide a distinctive look that consumers would find more appealing—all for the same price as the present packaging.

Sonoco chose to include a point of parity in its value proposition because, in this case, the customer would not even consider a packaging redesign if the price went up. The first point of difference in the value proposition (increased efficiency) delivered cost savings to the customer, allowing it to move from a seven-day, three-shift production schedule during peak times to a five-day, two-shift operation. The second point of difference delivered an advantage at the consumer level, helping the customer to grow its revenues and profits incrementally. In persuading the customer to change to the redesigned packaging, Sonoco did not neglect to mention the other favorable points of difference. Rather, it chose to place much greater emphasis on the two points of difference and the one point of parity that mattered most to the customer, thereby delivering a value proposition with resonating focus.

Stressing as a point of parity what customers may mistakenly presume to be a point of difference favoring a competitor's offering can be one of the most important parts of constructing an effective value proposition. Take the case of Intergraph, an Alabama-based provider of engineering software to engineering, procurement, and construction firms. One software product that Intergraph offers, SmartPlant P&ID, enables customers to define flow processes for valves, pumps, and piping within plants they are designing and generate piping and instrumentation diagrams (P&ID). Some prospective customers wrongly presume that SmartPlant's drafting performance would not be as good as that of the next best alternative, because the alternative is built on computer-aided design (CAD), a better-known drafting tool than the relational database platform on which SmartPlant is built. So Intergraph tackled the perception head on, gathering data from reference customers to substantiate that this point of contention was actually a point of parity.

Here's how the company played it. Intergraph's resonating focus value proposition for this software consisted of one point of parity (which the customer initially thought was a point of contention), followed by three points of difference:

> *Point of parity:* Using this software, customers can create P&ID graphics (either drawings or reports) as fast, if not faster, as they can using CAD, the next best alternative.
>
> *Point of difference:* This software checks all of the customer's upstream and downstream data related to plant assets and procedures, using universally accepted engineering practices, company-specific rules, and project- or process-specific rules at each stage of the design process, so that

Case in Point: Transforming a Weak Value Proposition

A leading supplier of specialty resins used in architectural coatings—such as paint for buildings—recognized that its customers were coming under pressure to comply with increasingly strict environmental regulations. At the same time, the supplier reasoned, no coating manufacturer would want to sacrifice performance. So the resins supplier developed a new type of high-performance resins that would enable its customers to comply with stricter environmental standards—albeit at a higher price but with no reduction in performance.

In its initial discussions with customers who were using the product on a trial basis, the resins supplier was surprised by the tepid reaction it received, particularly from commercial managers. They were not enthusiastic about the sales prospects for higher-priced coatings with commercial painting contractors, the primary target market. They would not, they said, move to the new resin until regulation mandated it.

Taken aback, the resins supplier decided to conduct customer value research to better understand the requirements and preferences of its customers' customers and how the performance of the new resin would affect their total cost of doing business. The resins supplier went so far as to study the requirements and preferences of the commercial painting contractors' customers—building owners. The supplier conducted a series of focus groups and field tests with painting contractors to gather data. The performance on primary customer requirements—such as coverage,

---

the customer avoids costly mistakes such as missing design change interdependencies or, worse, ordering the wrong equipment.

Point of difference: This software is integrated with upstream and downstream tasks, such as

dry time, and durability—was studied, and customers were asked to make performance trade-offs and indicate their willingness to pay for coatings that delivered enhanced performance. The resins supplier also joined a commercial painting contractor industry association, enrolled managers in courses on how contractors are taught to estimate jobs, and trained the staff to work with the job-estimation software used by painting contractors.

Several insights emerged from this customer value research. Most notable was the realization that only 15% of a painting contractor's costs are the coatings; labor is by far the largest cost component. If a coating could provide greater productivity—for example, a faster drying time that allowed two coats to be applied during a single eight-hour shift—contractors would likely accept a higher price.

The resins supplier retooled its value proposition from a single dimension, environmental regulation compliance, to a resonating focus value proposition where environmental compliance played a significant but minor part. The new value proposition was "The new resin enables coatings producers to make architectural coatings with higher film build and gives the painting contractors the ability to put on two coats within a single shift, thus increasing painter productivity while also being environmentally compliant." Coatings customers enthusiastically accepted this value proposition, and the resins supplier was able to get a 40% price premium for its new offering over the traditional resin product.

process simulation and instrumentation design, thus requiring no reentry of data (and reducing the margin for error).

Point of difference: With this software, the customer is able to link remote offices to execute the project and then merge the pieces into a single deliverable database to hand to its customer, the facility owner.

Resonating focus value propositions are very effective, but they're not easy to craft: Suppliers must undertake customer value research to gain the insights to construct them. Despite all of the talk about customer value, few suppliers have actually done customer value research, which requires time, effort, persistence, and some creativity. But as the best practices we studied highlight, thinking through a resonating focus value proposition disciplines a company to research its customers' businesses enough to help solve their problems. As the experience of a leading resins supplier amply illustrates, doing customer value research pays off. (See the sidebar "Case in Point: Transforming a Weak Value Proposition.")

Substantiate Customer Value Propositions

In a series of business roundtable discussions we conducted in Europe and the United States, customer managers reported that "We can save you money!" has become almost a generic value proposition from prospective suppliers. But, as one participant in Rotterdam wryly observed, most of the suppliers were telling "fairy tales." After he heard a pitch from a prospective supplier, he would follow up with a series of questions to determine whether the supplier had the people, processes, tools, and experience to actually save his firm money. As often as not, they could not really back up the claims. Simply put, to make customer value propositions persuasive, suppliers must be able to demonstrate and document them.

Value word equations enable a supplier to show points of difference and points of contention relative to the next best alternative, so that customer managers can easily grasp them and find them persuasive. A value word equation expresses in words and simple mathematical operators (for example, + and ÷) how to assess the differences in functionality or performance between a supplier's offering and the next best alternative and how to convert those differences into dollars.

Best-practice firms like Intergraph and, in Milwaukee, Rockwell Automation use value word equations to make it clear to customers how their offerings will lower costs or add value relative to the next best alternatives. The data needed to provide the value estimates are most often collected from the customer's business operations by supplier and customer managers working together, but, at times, data may come from outside sources, such as industry association studies. Consider a value word equation that Rockwell Automation used to calculate the cost savings from reduced power usage that a customer would gain by using a Rockwell Automation motor solution instead of a competitor's comparable offering:

Power Reduction Cost Savings

$= [\text{kW spent} \times \text{number of operating hours per year} \times \text{\$ per kW hour} \times \text{number of years system solution in operation}]_{\text{Competitor Solution}}$

$- [\text{kW spent} \times \text{number of operating hours per year} \times \text{\$ per kW hour} \times \text{number of years system solution in operation}]_{\text{Rockwell Automation Solution}}$

This value word equation uses industry-specific terminology that suppliers and customers in business markets rely on to communicate precisely and efficiently about functionality and performance.

Demonstrate Customer Value in Advance

Prospective customers must see convincingly the cost savings or added value they can expect from using the supplier's offering instead of the next best alternative. Best-practice suppliers, such as Rockwell Automation and precision-engineering and manufacturing firm Nijdra Groep in the Netherlands, use *value case histories* to demonstrate this. Value case histories document the cost savings or added value that reference customers have actually received from their use of the supplier's market offering. Another way that best-practice firms, such as Pennsylvania-based GE Infrastructure Water & Process Technologies (GEIW&PT) and SKF USA, show the value of their offerings to prospective customers in advance is through *value calculators*. These customer value assessment tools typically are spreadsheet software applications that salespeople or value specialists use on laptops as part of a consultative selling approach to demonstrate the value that customers likely would receive from the suppliers' offerings.

When necessary, best-practice suppliers go to extraordinary lengths to demonstrate the value of their offerings relative to the next best alternatives. The polymer chemicals unit of Akzo Nobel in Chicago recently conducted an on-site two-week pilot on a production reactor at a prospective customer's facility to gather data firsthand on the performance of its high-purity metal organics offering relative to the next best alternative in producing compound semiconductor wafers. Akzo Nobel paid this prospective customer for these two weeks, in which each day was a trial because of daily considerations such as output and maintenance. Akzo Nobel now has data from an actual production machine to substantiate assertions about its product and anticipated cost savings, and evidence that the compound semiconductor wafers produced are as good as or better than those the customer currently grows using the next best alternative. To let its prospective clients' customers verify this for themselves, Akzo Nobel brought them sample wafers it had produced for testing. Akzo Nobel combines this point of parity with two points of difference: significantly lower energy costs for conversion and significantly lower maintenance costs.

Document Customer Value

Demonstrating superior value is necessary, but this is no longer enough for a firm to be considered a best-practice company. Suppliers also must document the cost savings and incremental profits (from additional revenue generated) their offerings deliver to the companies that have purchased them. Thus, suppliers work with their customers to define how cost savings or incremental profits will be tracked and then, after a suitable period of time, work with customer managers to document the results. They use value documenters to further refine their customer value models, create value case histories, enable customer managers to get credit for the cost savings and incremental profits produced, and (because customer managers know that the supplier is willing to return later to document the value received) enhance the credibility of the offering's value.

A pioneer in substantiating value propositions over the past decade, GEIW&PT documents the results provided to customers through its value generation planning (VGP) process and tools, which enable its field personnel to understand customers' businesses and to plan, execute, and document projects that have the highest value impact for its customers. An online tracking tool allows GEIW&PT and customer managers to easily monitor the execution and documented results of each project the company undertakes. Since it began using VGP in 1992, GEIW&PT has documented more than 1,000 case histories, accounting for $1.3 billion in customer cost savings, 24 billion gallons of water conserved, 5.5 million tons of waste eliminated, and 4.8 million tons of air emissions removed.

As suppliers gain experience documenting the value provided to customers, they become knowledgeable about how their offerings deliver superior value to customers and even how the value delivered varies across kinds of customers. Because of this extensive and detailed knowledge, they become confident in predicting the cost savings and added value that prospective customers likely will receive. Some best-practice suppliers are even willing to guarantee a certain amount of savings before a customer signs on.

A global automotive engine manufacturer turned to Quaker Chemical, a Pennsylvania-based specialty chemical and management services firm, for help in significantly reducing its operating costs. Quaker's team of chemical, mechanical, and environmental engineers, which has been meticulously documenting cost savings to customers for years, identified potential savings for this customer through process and productivity improvements. Then Quaker implemented its proposed solution—with a guarantee that savings would be five times more than what the engine manufacturer spent annually just to purchase coolant. In real numbers, that meant savings of $1.4 million a year. What customer wouldn't find such a guarantee persuasive?

Superior Business Performance

We contend that customer value propositions, properly constructed and delivered, make a significant contribution to business strategy and performance. GE Infrastructure Water & Process Technologies' recent development of a new service offering to refinery customers illustrates how general manager John Panichella allocates limited resources to initiatives that will generate the greatest incremental value for his company and its customers. For example, a few years ago, a field rep had a creative idea for a new product, based on his comprehensive understanding of refinery processes and how refineries make money. The field rep submitted a new product introduction (NPI) request to the hydrocarbon industry marketing manager for further study. Field reps or anyone else in the organization can submit NPI requests whenever they have an inventive idea for a customer solution that they believe would have a large value impact but that GEIW&PT presently does not offer. Industry marketing managers, who have extensive industry expertise, then perform scoping studies to understand the potential of the proposed products to deliver significant value to segment customers. They create business cases for the proposed product, which are "racked and stacked" for review. The senior management team of GEIW&PT sort through a large number of potential initiatives competing for limited resources. The team approved Panichella's initiative, which led to the development of a new offering that provided refinery customers with documented cost savings amounting to five to ten times the price they paid for the offering, thus realizing a compelling value proposition.

Sonoco, at the corporate level, has made customer value propositions fundamental to its business strategy. Since 2003, its CEO, Harris DeLoach, Jr., and the executive committee have set an ambitious growth goal for the firm: sustainable, double-digit, profitable growth every year. They believe that distinctive value propositions are crucial to support the growth initiative. At Sonoco, each value proposition must be:

- *Distinctive.* It must be superior to those of Sonoco's competition.

- *Measurable.* All value propositions should be based on tangible points of difference that can be quantified in monetary terms.

- *Sustainable.* Sonoco must be able to execute this value proposition for a significant period of time.

Unit managers know how critical DVPs are to business unit performance because they are one of the ten key metrics on the managers' performance scorecard. In senior management reviews, each unit manager presents proposed value propositions for each target market segment or key customer, or both. The managers then receive summary feedback on the value proposition metric (as well as on each of the nine other performance metrics) in terms of whether their proposals can lead to profitable growth.

In addition, Sonoco senior management tracks the relationship between business unit value propositions and business unit performance—and, year after year, has concluded that the emphasis on DVPs has made a significant contribution toward sustainable, double-digit, profitable growth.

Best-practice suppliers recognize that constructing and substantiating resonating focus value propositions is not a onetime undertaking, so they make sure their people know how to identify what the next value propositions ought to be. Quaker Chemical, for example, conducts a value-proposition training program each year for its chemical program managers, who work on-site with customers and have responsibility for formulating and executing customer value propositions. These managers first review case studies from a variety of industries Quaker serves, where their peers have executed savings projects and quantified the monetary savings produced. Competing in teams, the managers then participate in a simulation where they interview "customer managers" to gather information needed to devise a proposal for a customer value proposition. The team that is judged to have the best proposal earns "bragging rights," which are highly valued in Quaker's competitive culture. The training program, Quaker believes, helps sharpen the skills of chemical program managers to identify savings projects when they return to the customers they are serving.

As the final part of the training program, Quaker stages an annual real-world contest where the chemical program managers have 90 days to submit a proposal for a savings project that they plan to present to their customers. The director of chemical management judges these proposals and provides feedback. If he deems a proposed project to be viable, he awards the manager with a gift certificate. Implementing these projects goes toward fulfilling Quaker's guaranteed annual savings commitments of, on average, $5 million to $6 million a year per customer.

Each of these businesses has made customer value propositions a fundamental part of its business strategy. Drawing on best practices, we have presented an approach to customer value propositions that businesses can implement to communicate, with resonating focus, the superior value their offerings provide to target market segments and customers. Customer value propositions can be a guiding beacon as well as the cornerstone for superior business performance. Thus, it is the responsibility of senior management and general management, not just marketing management, to ensure that their customer value propositions are just that.

JAMES C. ANDERSON is the William L. Ford Distinguished Professor of Marketing and Wholesale Distribution at Northwestern's Kellogg School of Management. **JAMES A. NARUS** is a professor of business marketing at Wake Forest University in North Carolina. **WOUTER VAN ROSSUM** is a professor of commercial and strategic management at the University of Twente, The Netherlands.

Originally published in March 2006. Reprint R0603F

Getting Brand Communities Right

by Susan Fournier and Lara Lee

IN 1983, HARLEY-DAVIDSON FACED extinction. Twenty-five years later, the company boasted a top-50 global brand valued at $7.8 billion. Central to the company's turnaround, and to its subsequent success, was Harley's commitment to building a brand community: a group of ardent consumers organized around the lifestyle, activities, and ethos of the brand.

Inspired by Harley's results and enabled by Web 2.0 technologies, marketers in industries from packaged goods to industrial equipment are busy trying to build communities around their own brands. Their timing is right. In today's turbulent world, people are hungry for a sense of connection; and in lean economic times, every company needs new ways to do more with what it already has. Unfortunately, although many firms aspire to the customer loyalty, marketing efficiency, and brand authenticity that strong communities deliver, few understand what it takes to achieve such benefits. Worse, most subscribe to serious misconceptions about what brand communities are and how they work.

On the basis of our combined 30 years of researching, building, and leveraging brand communities, we identify and dispel seven commonly held myths about maximizing their value for a firm. For companies considering a community strategy, we offer cautionary tales and design principles. For those with existing brand communities, we provide new approaches for increasing their impact. And as you'll see from our discussion and the online "Community Readiness Audit" at brandcommunity.hbr.org, your decision is not whether a community is right for your brand. It's whether you're willing to do what's needed to get a brand community right.

Myth #1

A brand community is a marketing strategy.

The Reality

A brand community is a business strategy.

Too often, companies isolate their community-building efforts within the marketing function. That is a mistake. For a brand community to yield maximum benefit, it must be framed as a high-level strategy supporting businesswide goals.

Harley-Davidson provides a quintessential example. Following the 1985 leveraged buy-back that saved the company, management completely reformulated the

Idea in Brief

Hooray for brand communities—those groups of ardent consumers organized around a brand's lifestyle (think Harley-Davidson devotees and Playstation gamers). Brand-community members buy more, remain loyal, and reduce marketing costs through grassroots evangelism.

But many companies mismanage their brand communities because executives hold false beliefs about how to use these communities to create value. For example, they believe companies should tightly control such communities.

In truth, brand communities generate more value when *members* control them—and when companies create conditions in which communities can thrive. For instance, Vans—a skateboarding shoe manufacturer—had long invited lead users to co-design products, fostering a strong brand community as a result. When privately owned skateboarding parks began closing, Vans supported its community by opening its own park.

---

competitive strategy and business model around a brand community philosophy. Beyond just changing its marketing programs, Harley-Davidson re-tooled every aspect of its organization—from its culture to its operating procedures and governance structure—to drive its community strategy.

Harley management recognized that the brand had developed as a community-based phenomenon. The "brotherhood" of riders, united by a shared ethos, offered Harley the basis for a strategic repositioning as the one motorcycle manufacturer that understood bikers on their own terms. To reinforce this community-centric positioning and solidify the connection between the company and its customers, Harley staffed all community-outreach events with employees rather than

Idea in Practice

Additional truths about brand communities:

Brand community is a business—not a marketing—strategy.

Don't isolate your community-building efforts within your marketing function. Instead, ensure these efforts support businesswide goals by integrating them into your company's overall strategy.

Example: Harley-Davidson reformulated its competitive strategy around brand community. For instance, all community-outreach events are staffed by employees, not freelance contractors. Many employees become riders; many riders join the company.

Brand communities exist to serve their member's needs—not your business.

Members have many community-related needs—including cultivating interests, expanding networks, and relaxing in a safe haven. Discern these needs, then help community members fulfill them.

Example: "Third Place" brands like Gold's Gym and Starbucks tap into the need for social links by providing venues that foster personal interaction.

Strong brands arise from the right community structure—not vice versa.

The strongest, most stable structure for a brand community is a "web" whose affiliations are based on close one-to-one connections. To cultivate webs, provide opportunities for members to forge many interpersonal links.

Example: The Harley-Davidson Museum fosters personal connections through programs like the Rivet Wall, where people order custom-engraved rivets that are installed on decorative walls around the museum campus. Visitors viewing their own and others' rivets start chatting, often forging friendships.

---

hired hands. For employees, this regular, close contact with the people they served added such meaning to their work that the weekend out-reach assignments routinely attracted more volunteers than were needed. Many employees became riders, and many riders joined

Brand communities thrive on conflict and contrast—not love.

Communities are inherently political: "In-groups" need "out-groups" against which to define themselves. To strengthen group unity, create a sense of contrast, conflict, and boundaries.

Example: Dove's Campaign for Real Beauty brought "real women" (less-than-pretty, older, large, skinny) together worldwide to fight industry-imposed beauty ideals. The women formed in camaraderie around this mission.

Communities are strongest when all members—not just opinion leaders—have roles.

In strong communities, everyone plays a value-adding role. Roles include the Mentor (shares expertise with other members), Greeter (welcomes new members), and Storyteller (disseminates the community's history throughout the group).

To cultivate an enduring community, ensure that members can adopt new roles or switch roles as their lives change.

Example: Saddleback Church in Orange County, California, constantly monitors members' needs and creates new subgroups (such as personal financial planning) to keep people engaged.

Online social networks are only a tool—not your community strategy.

Many online interactions are shallow and transient, diluting the community overall. So use online tools selectively to support your brand community's needs.

Example: L'Oréal uses online tools (such as blogs) only with certain brands, such as mainstream Garnier, whose brand-community members value social interaction and view themselves as fighting for a better world.

the company. Executives were required to spend time in the field with customers and bring their insights back to the firm. This close-to-the-customer strategy was codified in Harley-Davidson's operating philosophy and rein-forced during new-employee orientations.

Decisions at all levels were grounded in the community perspective, and the company acknowledged the community as the rightful owner of the brand.

Harley's community strategy was also supported by a radical organizational redesign. Functional silos were replaced with senior leadership teams sharing decision-making responsibility across three imperatives: Create Demand, Produce Product, and Provide Support. Further, the company established a stand-alone organization reporting directly to the president to formalize and nurture the company-community relationship through the Harley Owners Group (H.O.G.) membership club. As a result of this organizational structure, community-building activities were treated not solely as marketing expenses but as companywide, COO-backed investments in the success of the business model.

Myth #2

A brand community exists to serve the business.

The Reality

A brand community exists to serve the people in it.

Managers often forget that consumers are actually people, with many different needs, interests, and responsibilities. A community-based brand builds loyalty not by driving sales transactions but by helping people meet their needs. Contrary to marketers' assumptions, however, the needs that brand communities can satisfy are not just about gaining status or trying on a new identity through brand affiliation. People participate in communities for a wide variety of reasons—to find emotional support and en-couragement, to explore ways to contribute to the greater good, and to cultivate interests and skills, to name a few. For members, brand communities are a means to an end, not an end in themselves.

Outdoorseiten offers an extreme example of how the needs of a community can actually give rise to a brand. The European website outdoorseiten.net originated as a venue where hiking and camping enthusiats could exchange information about their shared life-style: Where is a good place to hike with children? Which shoes are best for rocky terrain? Members collaborated in order to gain access to the resources and skills they needed to accomplish their goals. Eventually, the community created its own Outdoorseiten brand of tents and backpacks. The community's brand grew not from a need to express a shared identity but from a desire to meet members' specialized needs.

Often, people are more interested in the social links that come from brand affiliations than they are in the brands themselves. They join communities to build new relationships. Facebook provides a straightforward example, but country clubs and churches reveal similar dynamics. "Third place" brands such as Gold's Gym and Starbucks tap into this by providing bricks-and-mortar venues that foster interaction. In such instances, brand loyalty is the reward for meeting people's needs for community, not the impetus for the community to form.

Robust communities are built not on brand reputation but on an understanding of members' lives. Pepperidge

Farm learned this lesson when its initial community effort—a website stocked with Goldfish-branded kids games—met with little success. Taking a step back from its brand-centric execution to identify areas where kids and parents really needed help, the Goldfish team uncovered alarming statistics about depression and low self-esteem among children. Partnering with psychologist Karen Reivich of the Positive Psychology Center at the University of Pennsylvania, managers recently launched an online community, fishfulthinking.com, that repackages academic research about failure, frustration, hopefulness, and emotional awareness into learning activities and discussion tools designed to help parents develop resiliency in their kids. Putting the brand second is tough for a marketer to do, but it's essential if a strong community is the goal.

Myth #3

Build the brand, and the community will follow.

The Reality

Engineer the community, and the brand will be strong.

Strategy consultancy Jump Associates has identified three basic forms of community affiliation: pools, webs, and hubs (see the exhibit "Three forms of community affiliation"). Effective community strategies combine all three in a mutually reinforcing system.

Members of *pools* are united by shared goals or values (think Republicans, Democrats, or Apple devotees).

Three forms of community affiliation

People have strong associations with a shared activity or goal, or shared values, and loose associations with one another.

The shared activity, goal, or values are the key to this community affiliation.

Examples:
- Apple enthusiasts
- Republicans or Democrats
- Ironman triathletes

People have strong one-to-one relationships with others who have similar or complementary needs.

Personal relationships are the key to this community affiliation.

Examples:
- Facebook
- Cancer Survivors Network
- Hash House Harriers

People have strong connections to a central figure and weaker associations with one another

A charismatic figure is the key to this community affiliation.

Examples:
- Deepak Chopra
- Hannah Montana
- Oprah

Decades of brand management theory have schooled managers in a pool-based approach to brand building: Identify and consistently communicate a clear set of values that emotionally connect consumers with the brand. Unfortunately, pools deliver only limited community benefits—people share a set of abstract beliefs but build few interpersonal relationships. Further, the common meaning that holds members together often becomes diluted if the brand attempts to grow. Unless the affiliation to a brand idea is supplemented with human connections, community members are at risk of dropping out. The solution lies in using webs and hubs to strengthen and expand the community.

Web affiliations are based on strong one-to-one connections (think social networking sites or the Cancer Survivors Network). Webs are the strongest and most stable form of community because the people in them are bound by many and varied relationships. The Harley-Davidson Museum, for example, builds webs of interpersonal connections through features such as walls around the campus decorated with large, custom-inscribed stainless-steel rivets commissioned by individuals or groups. As museum visitors read the inscriptions on the rivets, they reflect on the stories and people behind them. People who meet at the rivet walls soon find themselves comparing interesting inscriptions, and before long they're engaged in conversation, planning to stay in touch and perhaps even share a ride someday. Through rivet walls and other means of fostering interpersonal connections, the museum strengthens the Harley-Davidson brand pool by building webs within it.

Members of *hubs* are united by their admiration of an individual (think Deepak Chopra or Hannah Montana). The hub is a strong albeit unstable form of community that often breaks apart once the central figure is no longer present. But hubs can help communities acquire new members who hold similar values. Harley-Davidson, for instance, built a bridge to a younger audience through its association with professional skateboarder and Harley enthusiast Heath Kirchart. Hubs can also be used to create or strengthen a brand pool, a strategy Nike has used since its inception by associating with stars such as Michael Jordan and Tiger Woods. To build stable communities, hub connections must be bonded to the community through webs. With its Nike+ online community, which cultivates peer-to-peer support and interaction by encouraging members to challenge and trash-talk one another, Nike has found a brand-appropriate way of creating webs to strengthen its pool and hubs.

Myth #4

Brand communities should be love-fests for faithful brand advocates.

The Reality

Smart companies embrace the conflicts that make communities thrive.

Most companies prefer to avoid conflict. But communities are inherently political, and conflict is the norm. "In" groups need "out" groups against which to define themselves. PlayStation gamers dismiss Xbox. Apple enthusiasts hate Microsoft and Dell. Dunkin' Donuts coffee drinkers shun Starbucks. Dividing lines are fundamental even within communities, where perceived degrees of passion and loyalty separate the hard-core fans from the poseurs. Community is all about rivalries and lines drawn in the sand.

Dove's much-lauded "Campaign for Real Beauty" offers a vivid example of how companies can use conflict to their advantage. The campaign brought "real women" together worldwide to stand up against industry-imposed beauty ideals. Older women, large women, skinny women, and less-than-pretty women united in camaraderie against a common foe. Dove identified a latent "out" group and claimed it for its brand.

Firms can reinforce rivalries directly or engage others to fan the flames. Pepsi, renowned for taking on rival Coca-Cola in the orginal Pepsi Challenge, is now running advertising starring lackluster Coke drinkers in dingy retirement homes. Apple's PC-versus-Mac ads sparked not only Microsoft's "I am a PC" countercampaign but also a host of You Tube parodies from both camps. A group's unity is strengthened when such conflicts and contrasts are brought to the fore.

Some companies make the mistake of attempting to smooth things over. Porsche's 2002 launch of the Cayenne SUV provides an instructive case in point. Owners of 911 models refused to accept the Cayenne as a "real" Porsche. They argued that it did not have the requisite racing heritage and painted Cayenne drivers as soccer moms who did not and could not understand the brand. Die-hard Porsche owners even banned Cayenne owners from rennlist.com, a site that started as a discussion board for Porsche enthusiasts and has grown to include pages devoted to Audi, BMW, and Lamborghini. The company attempted to mend the rift through a television campaign, complete with roaring engines at a metaphorical starting gate, aimed at demonstrating that the Cayenne was a genuine member of the Porsche family. The entrenched community was not convinced. Positioning the Cayenne as a race car was "a stretch that only delusional Porsche marketers could possibly attempt—and a flat-out insult to every great Porsche sports car that has come before it," one person wrote on autoextremist.com. Smart managers know that singing around the campfire will not force warring tribes to unite. Communities become stronger by highlighting, not erasing, the boundaries that define them.

Myth #5

Opinion leaders build strong communities.

The Reality

Communities are strongest when everyone plays a role.
   Opinion leaders and evangelists play important and well-documented roles in social networks. They spread information, influence decisions, and help new ideas gain traction. But whereas focusing on opinion leaders may be sage advice for buzz campaigns, it is a misguided approach to community building. Robust communities

establish cultural bedrock by enabling every-one to play a valuable role.

From our examination of research on communities including the Red Hat Society, Burning Man, Trekkies, and MGB car clubs, we have identified 18 social and cultural roles critical to community function, preservation, and evolution (see the exhibit "Common community roles"). These include performers, supporters, mentors, learners, heroes, talent scouts, and historians, to name a few. In complementary research, Hope Schau of the University of Arizona and Eric Arnould of the University of Wyoming have documented 11 value-creation practices among community members, including evangelizing, customizing, welcoming, badging, competing, and empathizing. Companies with existing communities can evaluate the roles and behaviors currently being demonstrated and identify gaps that could be filled to improve community function. Those designing new communities can create structures and support systems to ensure the availability of a wide range of roles.

Recognizing that life changes often prompt people to reevaluate their affiliations, successful communities give members opportunities to take on new roles, alternate between roles, and negotiate tensions across roles in conflict—without ever leaving the fold. Non-profit communities are particularly good in this respect. Saddleback Church of Orange County, California, maintains a cohesive community despite membership of over 20,000 by constantly monitoring individuals'

Common community roles

Members of strong brand communities stay involved and add value by playing a wide variety of roles. In designing a new community or strengthening an existing one, companies should incorporate an assortment of roles into the community structure and help members take on new roles as their needs change. Below are 18 roles critical to a community's function, preservation, and evolution.

Mentor: Teaches others and shares expertise

Learner: Enjoys learning and seeks self-improvement

Back-up: Acts as a safety net for others when they try new things

Partner: Encourages, shares, and motivates

Storyteller: Spreads the community's story throughout the group

Historian: Preserves community memory; codifies rituals and rites

Hero: Acts as a role model within the community

Celebrity: Serves as a figurehead or icon of what the community represents

Decision Maker: Makes choices affecting the community's structure and function

Provider: Hosts and takes care of other members

Greeter: Welcomes new members into the community

Guide: Helps new members navigate the culture

Catalyst: Introduces members to new people and ideas

Performer: Takes the spotlight

Supporter: Participates passively as an audience for others

Ambassador: Promotes the community to outsiders

Accountant: Keeps track of people's participation

Talent Scout: Recruits new members

---

needs and creating subgroups and roles to keep people engaged. Groups are organized not only by age, gender, and interests, but also by shared challenges, social commitments, and family situations. People are offered many types of roles, from active to passive, in small groups and large, and can participate in person, by phone, or online. Assorted print and digital tools help people identify options and map opportunities, so they can easily change roles or try on new ones.

Myth #6

Online social networks are the key to a community strategy.

The Reality

Online networks are just one tool, not a community strategy.

Forming an online community is often a knee-jerk reaction to the CEO's demand for a Web 2.0 strategy. Online social networks get lots of buzz, and given today's enabling technologies it seems silly to pass up opportunities in the virtual world. Unfortunately, most company-sponsored online "communities" are nothing more than far-flung focus groups established in the hope that consumers will bond around the virtual suggestion box. There's nothing wrong with listening to customers, but this isn't a community strategy.

Online social networks can serve valuable community functions. They help people find rich solutions to ambiguous problems and serendipitous connections to people and ideas. Yet even a well-crafted networking site has limitations. The anonymity of web encounters often emboldens antisocial behavior, and the shallow, transient nature of many online interactions results in weak social bonds. And, lest we forget, a huge chunk of life still takes place off-line. Physical spaces play important roles in fostering community connections. According to Mark Rosenbaum of Northern Illinois University, communities that are developed in third places like gyms and coffee shops often provide social and emotional support equal to or stronger than family ties—a benefit that delivers price premiums of up to 20%.

Smart marketers use online tools selectively to support community needs. L'Oréal strikes the right balance with its methodical approach. The company maps its brands along two dimensions: (1) brands of authority versus brands of conversation, and (2) mainstream versus niche brands. Each cell in the grid suggests a different community approach. Brands of authority offer expert affiliation and advice. L'Oréal (the company's mainstream brand of authority) builds community through heavy TV advertising featuring celebrity spokespeople to inspire hub affiliations. La Roche-Posay (a niche brand of authority) nurtures a worldwide community of dermatologists, both online and face-to-face, to expertly represent the brand. Brands of conversation thrive on social interaction and engagement. L'Oréal's Garnier (the company's mainstream brand of conversation) enlists well-known bloggers to share what they're doing to make the world a better place, using these hub figures to strengthen the brand's pool. Kiehl's (a niche brand of conversation) uses a grassroots focus on local charity sponsorships, in-store customer bulletin boards, and required employee volunteerism in the surrounding community to create the social glue. Although the tactics vary, the goal of L'Oréal's community-building strategies is always to connect with the people who make up the community in ways that reaffirm the essence of the brand.

Myth #7

Successful brand communities are tightly managed and controlled.

The Reality

Of and by the people, communities defy managerial control.

Excessive control has been the norm when it comes to community management. From Coca-Cola's pulling of its beloved soda off the shelves in 1985, to Microsoft's stifling of internal blogger Robert Scoble, to Hasbro's suing of fans for publishing content based on its brands, community managers tend to put corporate interests over those of their customers.

Such efforts have led to vigorous debate about how much control to assert over brand communities. That is the wrong question. Brand communities are not corporate assets, so control is an illusion. But relinquishing control does not mean abdicating responsibility. Effective brand stewards participate as community cocreators—nurturing and facilitating communities by creating the conditions in which they can thrive.

Vans, the famed maker of skateboarding shoes, has proved adept at building community through support rather than control. From the beginning, the company recognized its fan base of customers as the owners of its brand. Its self-appointed role was to stay close enough to the fans to understand where they were headed and then pursue the directions that would strengthen the community. From its earliest days, Vans worked with lead users within each of its sports communities to codesign new products. When privately owned skate parks began closing, Vans took care of enthusiasts by opening its own. Vans originally sponsored the Warped Tour, a traveling music festival appealing to young adults, as a way to support its customers' love of music. Later, realizing that amateur skateboarders were lacking a national championship event, Vans persuaded Warped Tour organizers to add one to their lineup and then acquired the Tour outright once it became a major celebration of skateboarding and bicycle motocross (BMX) culture. Warped Tour innovations now include air-conditioned "parental day care" lounges at tour stops to make it easier for young fans to attend, and an online community that supports year-round connections among fans and helps far-flung friends coordinate tour attendance.

Companies build effective communities through a design philosophy that replaces control with a balance of structure and flexibility. Jump Associates has identified nine archetypal community scripts that can be used as a framework for such design (see the exhibit "A sampling of community scripts"). A script is a set of expected behaviors in a particular social situation. Think, for example, of the script you'd follow for a date at a fancy

A sampling of community scripts

A script suggests a set of behaviors that are appropriate for a particular situation. Companies can design brand communities by establishing and reinforcing a base script and then layering on new scripts over time. Vans, a maker of skateboarding shoes, initially sold its products to tight-knit surfer and skateboarding communities. Building direct relationships with these groups and cultivating lead users within them reinforced an implicit Tribe script. By sponsoring competitions and skate parks, Vans introduced the Performance Space script. And through skateboarding clinics and demonstrations, the company added features of the Sewing Circle.

The Tribe

A group with deep interpersonal connections built through shared experiences, rituals, and traditions.

The Fort

An exclusive place for insiders to be safe and feel protected.

The Sewing Circle

A gathering at which people with common interests share experiences, provide support, and socialize.

The Patio

A semiprivate place that facilitates in-depth, meaningful connections.

The Bar

A public space that grants reliable although shallow connections.

The Tour Group

A way to participate in new experiences while staying inside a comfort zone.

The Performance Space

A place where members can be sure of finding an audience for their talents.

The Barn Raising

An effective way to accomplish tasks while socializing.

The Summer Camp

A periodic experience that reaffirms connections.

---

restaurant or a job interview in a CEO's office. Harley-Davidson offers a leading example of how to use scripts to build and enhance community. The Harley-Davidson brand ethos of the "brotherhood" is grounded in the script of the Tribe, in which deep social connections form through shared experiences and traditions. Management first reinforced this script to strengthen community identity and then gradually introduced elements of new scripts to enrich the experience over time. The Harley Owners Group introduced elements of the Fort (an exclusive place where insiders feel protected) through members-only events and special perks. Rallies and other recurring customer gatherings added the Summer Camp (a periodic experience that reaffirms connections). Both the Harley-Davidson Museum and dealerships were designed to leverage elements of the Patio (a semiprivate place that facilitates in-depth, meaningful connections) and the Bar (a public space that grants reliable but shallow connections) to foster different types of interpersonal connections. By layering those additional scripts over the Tribe foundation, Harley-Davidson was able to build multiple community experiences that appealed to different audiences while retaining a cohesive core.

Whether through constructive engagement, script-based design, or other means, smart companies define the terms of their community participation but discard their illusions of control.

Are You Ready?

Although any brand can benefit from a community strategy, not every company can pull it off. Executing community requires an organization-wide commitment and a willingness to work across functional boundaries. It takes the boldness to reexamine everything from company values to organizational design. And it takes the fortitude to meet people on their own terms, cede control, and accept conflict as part of the package. Is your organization up to the task? To find out, take our online "Community Readiness Audit" by visiting http://hbr.org/2009/04/getting-brand-communities-right/ar/1#.

Community is a potent strategy if it is approached with the right mind-set and skills. A strong brand community increases customer loyalty, lowers marketing costs, authenticates brand meanings, and yields an influx of ideas to grow the business. Through commitment, engagement, and support, companies can cultivate brand communities that deliver powerful returns. When you get community right, the benefits are irrefutable.

SUSAN FOURNIER is an associate professor of marketing at Boston University. **LARA LEE** is a member of the executive committee at Jump Associates, a strategy consulting firm in California.

Originally published in April 2009. Reprint R0904K

Aflac's CEO Explains How He Fell for the Duck

by Daniel P. Amos

THE AFLAC DUCK IS A rock star in Japan. That's the only way I can describe how big he has become there. In a down economy, Aflac Japan's sales increased by 12% in 2003, the year we introduced the duck. Today we insure one out of every four Japanese households and are the leading insurance company measured by number of policies in force. We took that title from Nippon Life, which had held it for more than 100 years.

In 2009 our Japanese marketing team introduced a new incarnation of the duck for a new insurance product. It's a mix of our duck and the traditional Asian good-luck white cat, Maneki Neko. The cat duck has become so popular that our newest commercial was voted number one in Japan. A giant plush version of Maneki Neko Duck toured the country by bus, drawing crowds as big as 20,000 in city after city. At each event we set up tables where we were able to sell policies to enthusiastic fans.

How did we even get to this point? What made our white duck a sensation in Japan when the original Aflac Duck commercial aired there? More important, how has it helped drive revenues up by 44% since 2003? Aflac's revenues in 2008 were $16.6 billion, with 70% of that coming from Japan.

No one is more surprised than I am.

Making a Name for Aflac

The Aflac Duck was created to increase the company's name recognition in the United States. When I first became CEO of the American Family Life Assurance Company, in 1990, I reviewed all of our operations and decided to sell or close the ones that were underperforming in order to focus on Japan and the United States, the two biggest insurance markets in the world. I took the $8 million we saved by closing those operations and launched a name-awareness ad campaign in the United States. Our name recognition at the time was about 2%. Nearly a decade later it was still below 10%. At that rate, I realized, I'd be retired before we reached 25%. We had to do something dramatic.

Keep in mind that the company's name was originally American Family Life Insurance Company. "Insurance" was changed to "assurance" as the result of a gentleman's coin toss between our former CEO and the head of a Wisconsin insurance company of the same name. But I could see that we still had trouble distinguishing ourselves from the scores of other companies

Idea in Brief

"The Aflac Duck is a rock star in Japan," writes the company CEO. From 2003, when the duck was introduced in that country, to 2008, Aflac's revenues increased by 44%, to $16.6 billion. Seventy percent of that increase came from Japan. This article tells the often comical story of how the duck came into existence in the United States, its instant success in CNN ads on New Year's Day in 2000, its transmogrification into a popular stuffed animal, and its export to Japan—where U.S. duck wranglers had to be flown in because the Japanese were unaccustomed to using live animals in commercials. In 2009 Aflac's Japanese marketing team introduced a new incarnation of the duck: Maneki Neko Duck, which incorporates the traditional Asian good-luck white cat. A giant plush version of the cat duck toured Japan by bus, drawing crowds as big as 20,000 in city after city. At each event the company set up tables where it sold policies to enthusiastic fans.

---

whose names began with "American." A radical name change would have been impractical, because we would have had to give up all our insurance licenses and reapply for new ones in every state. So rather than try a brand-new name, we decided to go with our acronym, Aflac.

In the late 1990s, we thought it was time for some new television advertisements, so we invited several agencies to pitch us at the same time in a creative shootout. We reviewed at least 20 different concepts and set out to test the best. The top two agencies were allowed to submit five ads each for testing.

One of the agencies was the New York–based Kaplan Thaler Group, whose creative guys came up with the idea of the Aflac Duck because they'd been having a hard time remembering our name. One day, one of them asked, "What's the name of the account we're pitching?" A colleague replied, "It's Aflac—Aflac—Aflac—Aflac." Someone said that he sounded like a duck, and the idea was born.

Kaplan Thaler decided to risk pitching the duck, hoping that we wouldn't be offended by the commercial's making fun of our name. With some trepidation, we agreed to let the agency test the commercial, along with some other concepts, to determine which of them was the most memorable.

Our previous commercials had consistently underperformed other financial services ads, which earned, on average, a 12—meaning that 12% of people polled recalled the company's name after watching the ad. In six years only one of our commercials had earned a 12.

In the Kaplan Thaler testing, one of the highest-scoring concepts featured the actor Ray Romano, whose hit television show, *Everybody Loves Raymond,* was then at the height of its popularity. At the end of the commercial, some children who were playing with blocks spelled out "Aflac." The ad scored an 18—more than 50% better than we had been doing. I considered it a bird in the hand.

But that darn Aflac Duck scored a 27.

We had a dilemma: Should we go with a commercial so bold—or with the gentle Ray Romano commercial that performed much better than our traditional ads? I asked one of my CEO friends, who said, "Nobody ever got fired for doing 50% better. Go with the safe choice."

But I couldn't ignore that 27.

A Duck in the Hand?

When I tried explaining to people what we were thinking about, no one got it. "Well, there's this duck," I'd say. "And he quacks *Aflac*." The response was always the same: a silent stare. So I stopped telling people. I didn't even tell our board; I just said we were trying something very bold and creative for our advertising campaign. It's difficult to explain, I told them, but we've had it tested, and the numbers are amazing.

Having gotten my college degree in risk management, I was committed to making the decision the way I'd been taught: Don't risk a lot for a little; don't risk more than you can afford to lose; and consider the odds. We were going to invest $1 million in the initial ad campaign. That's a lot of money, but we could afford to lose it, and I knew the odds. I decided that we'd run the commercial for two weeks and monitor every second. If it went badly, I was just going to pull it. At that time, we weren't sophisticated enough to realize exactly what we were doing. We were just going to test for name recognition afterward.

The first Aflac Duck ad debuted on New Year's Day, 2000, on CNN. It ran four times an hour. I knew that businesspeople would be watching CNN all day to see if the Y2K virus had wreaked havoc. So it was a great slot for us to gain maximum saturation. I watched it myself, over and over, still not sure if this would work.

Success was immediate—in fact, it was overwhelming. Our first day on the air, we had more visits to our website than in the entire year before. Within weeks we were getting requests for a stuffed-animal version of the duck. We didn't know how to manufacture ducks, but we quickly came up with a plan and decided that all the proceeds would be donated to the Aflac Cancer Center, in Atlanta. Within just a few months we had generated $75,000 for the cancer center.

I'm not sure I really believed that the duck was a success until a few months later. We were sponsoring an event at Disney Studios in connection with the Democratic National Convention in Los Angeles. We didn't know whether it would be a good idea to put ducks on all the tables—the kind of thing we'd ordinarily do as an event sponsor. This was a crowd of 500 movers and shakers. I didn't want to be embarrassed if no one took the ducks. I paid almost no attention to what anyone was talking about that afternoon; I was just watching to see if ducks were left on the tables.

By the end of the event, they were all gone. I spotted the head of Disney Studios with a bulge under his jacket. When I jokingly asked him what was going on, he said, "I want you to understand that Donald is always the king around here. But I want to take one home to my kids." That was it for me: the confirmation of confirmations. I knew we had a winner and we had to play it for all it was worth.

What remained to be seen, however, was whether we would achieve our business goals. That question was answered swiftly: In the first year our sales in the United States were up by 29%; in three years they had doubled. Our name recognition was up to 67% after two years of running the commercials. We increased our ad spending in proportion to growth. Today it's at $65 million, and our name recognition is higher than 90%.

The Duck Goes Global

When I decided it was time to bring the Aflac Duck to our Japanese market, I assumed, on the basis of the duck's tremendous success in the United States, that my idea would be eagerly received. But although I was excited about the notion of synergy and consistent global branding, our Japanese marketing director was not.

Aflac had been in Japan since 1974, and we were one of the most profitable companies operating there. But the marketing director felt no burning need to change his strategy. Although the Aflac Duck had become integral to who we were in the United States, he could not imagine that a white duck would sell insurance in Japan.

I'm not sure he understood the connection—maybe because in Japan a duck doesn't say "quack-quack," it says "ga-ga." Not to mention that in Japan the company was known by its full name: American Family Life Assurance Company. I began to understand the challenge for him. He did, however, halfheartedly agree to dub a U.S. commercial into Japanese and see how it did. Not surprisingly, it didn't do very well. I learned a valuable lesson from this experience: If you don't have buy-in from the people you're leading, your ideas won't work.

For a year and a half, I let my idea go. But it stuck in my mind. So I tried again. I told the marketing director that I wasn't going to force him to do this, but if he could find a way to make the duck work in Japan, I'd pay him a $50,000 bonus at the end of the year. Miraculously, angels must have come down and spoken to him, because lo and behold, he decided it might be a good idea to try the duck.

Once I had his buy-in, Aflac Japan helped make the appropriate cultural adjustments. First of all, the comedian Gilbert Gottfried's voice, which we used for the American duck, didn't work in Japan. People thought the duck was yelling at them. So we used a softer voice. And in the United States, people identify with the boisterous Aflac Duck who struggles to be heard. However, in Japan it's extremely rude to ignore people—or ducks, for that matter. So the Japanese duck interacts with people. He's a sage financial adviser who helps protect families.

Duck Wranglers Needed

Making a commercial in Japan with a real duck wasn't easy, because the Japanese weren't used to using live animals in ads. We had to fly in several people from our U.S. operation and a duck-wrangling crew for the commercial shoot. I'm pretty sure our Japanese colleagues thought we were *toppyoushimonai* (crazy) for doing all this. But they were committed to making it work in spite of their doubts.

The Japanese Aflac Duck ads exceeded our wildest expectations. Various versions of the jingle from the commercials became the number one downloaded

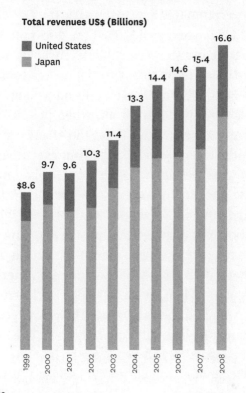

Growth in Aflac's two key markets 1999–2008

Since Aflac introduced the duck in its commercials, the company's combined revenues in the U.S. and Japan have markedly increased.

Source: Aflac

cell-phone ringtone in Japan. Following our lead in the United States—where the duck has a Twitter account and 165,000 Facebook fans, and YouTube is filled with parodies of Aflac commercials—Aflac Japan started marketing to the social media and created a website that allows people to rework the song the duck sings in Japanese commercials. In the website's first two months of existence, 100,000 people posted spoofs. (By early November 2009 that number had reached 200,000.)

So, how committed am I to the Aflac Duck? Well, in aid of branding, I wear only ties that have ducks on them. If I see a duck tie in a store, I buy it in every color. When we designed an addition to our corporate headquarters in Georgia, I told the architects that the only thing I insisted on was a duck pond. After all, when people came to headquarters, they wanted to see the Aflac Duck.

Recently, when I was talking to our executives in the United States, I described how the duck had morphed into a cat duck to introduce a new product in Japan. It reminded me of how, when I was first interviewed in Japan about our commercials, people asked me repeatedly to explain why we had picked a duck. I kept telling them that a duck says "quack-quack" in America. But no one got it. So I just started saying "Ducks are cute."

As I explained the cat duck to the U.S. executives, I had a similar feeling. All I could say was "Trust me, this works in Japan." By the end, every last one of them wanted a cat duck to take home. I swear, the Japanese are on to something with this cat duck campaign, but I haven't figured out how to make it work in the United States. I'll keep thinking.

DANIEL P. AMOS is the chairman and CEO of Aflac.

Originally published in January 2010. Reprint R1001L

Ending the War Between Sales and Marketing

by Philip Kotler, Neil Rackham, and Suj Krishnaswamy

PRODUCT DESIGNERS LEARNED YEARS ago that they'd save time and money if they consulted with their colleagues in manufacturing rather than just throwing new designs over the wall. The two functions realized it wasn't enough to just coexist—not when they could work together to create value for the company and for customers. You'd think that marketing and sales teams, whose work is also deeply interconnected, would have discovered something similar. As a rule, though, they're separate functions within an organization, and, when they do work together, they don't always get along. When sales are disappointing, Marketing blames the sales force for its poor execution of an otherwise brilliant rollout plan. The sales team, in turn, claims that Marketing sets prices too high and uses too much of the budget, which instead should go toward hiring more salespeople or paying the sales reps higher commissions. More broadly, sales departments tend to believe that marketers are out of touch with what's really going on with customers. Marketing believes the sales force is myopic—too focused on individual customer experiences, insufficiently aware of the larger market, and blind to the future. In short, each group often undervalues the other's contributions.

This lack of alignment ends up hurting corporate performance. Time and again, during research and consulting assignments, we've seen both groups stumble (and the organization suffer) because they were out of sync. Conversely, there is no question that, when Sales and Marketing work well together, companies see substantial improvement on important performance metrics: Sales cycles are shorter, market-entry costs go down, and the cost of sales is lower. That's what happened when IBM integrated its sales and marketing groups to create a new function called Channel Enablement. Before the groups were integrated, IBM senior executives Anil Menon and Dan Pelino told us, Sales and Marketing operated independent of one another. Salespeople worried only about fulfilling product demand, not creating it. Marketers failed to link advertising dollars spent to actual sales made, so Sales obviously couldn't see the value of marketing efforts. And, because the groups were poorly coordinated, Marketing's new product announcements often came at a time when Sales was not prepared to capitalize on them.

Curious about this kind of disconnect between Sales and Marketing, we conducted a study to identify best practices that could help enhance the joint performance

Idea in Brief

In too many companies, Sales and Marketing feud like Capulets and Montagues. Salespeople accuse marketers of being out of touch with what customers really want or setting prices too high. Marketers insist that salespeople focus too myopically on individual customers and short-term sales at the expense of longer-term profits.

Result? Poor coordination between the two teams—which only raises market-entry costs, lengthens sales cycles, and increases cost of sales.

How to get *your* sales and marketing teams to start working together? Kotler, Rackham, and Krishnaswamy recommend crafting a new relationship between them, one with the right degree of interconnection to tackle your most pressing business challenges.

For example, is your market becoming more commoditized or customized? If so, **align** Sales and Marketing through frequent, disciplined cross-functional communication and joint projects. Is competition becoming more complex than ever? Then fully **integrate** the teams, by having them share performance metrics and rewards and embedding marketers deeply in management of key accounts.

Create the *right* relationship between Sales and Marketing, and you reduce internecine squabbling, enabling these former combatants to boost top- *and* bottom-line growth, together.

and overall contributions of these two functions. We interviewed pairs of chief marketing officers and sales vice presidents to capture their perspectives. We looked in depth at the relationship between Sales and Marketing in a heavy equipment company, a materials company, a financial services firm, a medical systems company, an energy company, an insurance company, two high-tech electronic products companies, and an airline. Among our findings:

- The marketing function takes different forms in different companies at different product life-cycle

Idea in Practice

How interconnected should *your* Sales and Marketing teams be? The authors recommend determining their existing relationship, then strengthening interconnection if conditions warrant.

What's the Current Relationship?

The relationship is...	If sales and marketing...
Undefined	• Focus on their own tasks and agendas unless conflict arises between them. • Have developed independently. • Devote meetings between them to conflict resolution, not proactive collaboration.
Defined	• Have rules for preventing disputes. • Share a language for potentially contentious areas (e.g., defining a "lead"). • Use meetings to clarify mutual expectations.
Aligned	• Have clear but flexible boundaries: salespeople use marketing terminology; marketers participate in transactional sales. • Engage in joint planning and training.
Integrated	• Share systems, performance metrics, and rewards. • Behave as if they'll "rise or fall together."

Should You Create More Interconnection?

Strengthening Sales/Marketing interconnection isn't always necessary. For example, if your company is small and the teams operate independently while enjoying positive, informal relationships, don't interfere. The table offers guidelines for companies that *do* need change.

If the current relationship is...	and...	Then move the relationship to...	by...
Undefined	• Sales and Marketing have frequent conflicts and compete over resources. • Effort is duplicated, or tasks fall between the cracks.	Defined	• Creating clear rules of engagement, including hand-off points for important tasks (such as lead follow-up).
Defined	• The market is becoming commoditized or customized. • Product life cycles are shortening. • Despite clarified roles, efforts are still duplicated or tasks neglected.	Aligned	• Establishing regular meetings between Sales and Marketing to discuss major opportunities and problems. • Defining who should be consulted on which decisions (e.g., "Involve the brand manager in $2 million+ sales opportunities"). • Creating opportunities for Sales and Marketing to collaborate—for example, planning a conference together or rotating jobs.
Aligned	• The business landscape is marked by complexity and rapid change. • Marketing has split into upstream (strategic) and downstream (tactical) groups.	Integrated	• Having downstream marketers develop sales tools, help salespeople qualify leads, and use feedback from Sales to sell existing offerings to new market segments. • Evaluating and rewarding both teams' performance based on shared important metrics. For instance, establish a sales goal to which both teams commit. And define key sales metrics—such as number of new customers and closings—for salespeople *and* downstream marketers.

stages—all of which can deeply affect the relationship between Sales and Marketing.

- The strains between Sales and Marketing fall into two main categories: economic and cultural.

- It's not difficult for companies to assess the quality of the working relationship between Sales and Marketing. (This article includes a diagnostic tool for doing so.)

- Companies can take practical steps to move the two functions into a more productive relationship, once they've established where the groups are starting from.

Different Roles for Marketing

Before we look closely at the relationship between the two groups, we need to recognize that the nature of the marketing function varies significantly from company to company.

Most small businesses (and most businesses *are* small) don't establish a formal marketing group at all. Their marketing ideas come from managers, the sales force, or an advertising agency. Such businesses equate marketing with selling; they don't conceive of marketing as a broader way to position their firms.

Eventually, successful small businesses add a marketing person (or persons) to help relieve the sales force of some chores. These new staff members conduct research to calibrate the size of the market, choose the best markets and channels, and determine potential buyers' motives and influences. They work with outside agencies on advertising and promotions. They develop collateral materials to help the sales force attract customers and close sales. And, finally, they use direct mail, telemarketing, and trade shows to find and qualify leads for the sales force. Both Sales and Marketing see the marketing group as an adjunct to the sales force at this stage, and the relationship between the functions is usually positive.

As companies become larger and more successful, executives recognize that there is more to marketing than setting the four P's: product, pricing, place, and promotion. They determine that effective marketing calls for people skilled in segmentation, targeting, and positioning. Once companies hire marketers with those skills, Marketing becomes an independent player. It also starts to compete with Sales for funding. While the sales mission has not changed, the marketing mission has. Disagreements arise. Each function takes on tasks it believes the other should be doing but isn't. All too often, organizations find that they have a marketing function inside Sales, and a sales function inside Marketing. At this stage, the salespeople wish that the marketers would worry about future opportunities (long-term strategy) and leave the current opportunities (individual and group sales) to them.

Once the marketing group tackles higher-level tasks like segmentation, it starts to work more closely with other departments, particularly Strategic Planning, Product Development, Finance, and Manufacturing.

The company starts to think in terms of developing brands rather than products, and brand managers become powerful players in the organization. The marketing group is no longer a humble ancillary to the sales department. It sets its sights much higher: The marketers believe it's essential to transform the organization into a "marketing-led" company. As they introduce this rhetoric, others in the firm—including the sales group—question whether the marketers have the competencies, experience, and understanding to lead the organization.

While Marketing increases its influence within separate business units, it rarely becomes a major force at the corporate level. There are exceptions: Citigroup, Coca-Cola, General Electric, IBM, and Microsoft each have a marketing head at the corporate level. And Marketing is more apt to drive company strategy in major packaged-goods companies such as General Mills, Kraft, and Procter & Gamble. Even then, though, during economic downturns, Marketing is more closely questioned—and its workforce more likely to be cut—than Sales.

Why Can't They Just Get Along?

There are two sources of friction between Sales and Marketing. One is economic, and the other is cultural. The economic friction is generated by the need to divide the total budget granted by senior management to support Sales and Marketing. In fact, the sales force is apt to criticize how Marketing spends money on three of the four P's—pricing, promotion, and product. Take pricing. The marketing group is under pressure to achieve revenue goals and wants the sales force to "sell the price" as opposed to "selling through price." The salespeople usually favor lower prices because they can sell the product more easily and because low prices give them more room to negotiate. In addition, there are organizational tensions around pricing decisions. While Marketing is responsible for setting suggested retail or list prices and establishing promotional pricing, Sales has the final say over transactional pricing. When special low pricing is required, Marketing frequently has no input. The vice president of sales goes directly to the CFO. This does not make the marketing group happy.

Promotion costs, too, are a source of friction. The marketing group needs to spend money to generate customers' awareness of, interest in, preference for, and desire for a product. But the sales force often views the large sums spent on promotion—particularly on television advertising—as a waste of money. The VP of sales tends to think that this money would be better spent increasing the size and quality of the sales force.

When marketers help set the other P, the product being launched, salespeople often complain that it lacks the features, style, or quality their customers want. That's because the sales group's worldview is shaped by the needs of its individual customers. The marketing team, however, is concerned about releasing products whose features have broad appeal.

The budget for both groups also reflects which department wields more power within the organization, a significant factor. CEOs tend to favor the sales group when setting budgets. One chief executive told us, "Why should I invest in more marketing when I can get better results by hiring more salespeople?" CEOs often see sales as more tangible, with more short-run impact. The sales group's contributions to the bottom line are also easier to judge than the marketers' contributions.

The cultural conflict between Sales and Marketing is, if anything, even more entrenched than the economic conflict. This is true in part because the two functions attract different types of people who spend their time in very different ways. Marketers, who until recently had more formal education than salespeople, are highly analytical, data oriented, and project focused. They're all about building competitive advantage for the future. They judge their projects' performance with a cold eye, and they're ruthless with a failed initiative. However, that performance focus doesn't always look like action to their colleagues in Sales because it all happens behind a desk rather than out in the field. Salespeople, in contrast, spend their time talking to existing and potential customers. They're skilled relationship builders; they're not only savvy about customers' willingness to buy but also attuned to which product features will fly and which will die. They want to keep moving. They're used to rejection, and it doesn't depress them. They live for closing a sale. It's hardly surprising that these two groups of people find it difficult to work well together.

If the organization doesn't align incentives carefully, the two groups also run into conflicts about seemingly simple things—for instance, which products to focus on selling. Salespeople may push products with lower margins that satisfy quota goals, while Marketing wants them to sell products with higher profit margins and more promising futures. More broadly speaking, the two groups' performance is judged very differently. Salespeople make a living by closing sales, full stop. It's easy to see who (and what) is successful—almost immediately. But the marketing budget is devoted to programs, not people, and it takes much longer to know whether a program has helped to create long-term competitive advantage for the organization.

Four Types of Relationships

Given the potential economic and cultural conflicts, one would expect some strains to develop between the two groups. And, indeed, some level of dysfunction usually

---

How well do Sales and Marketing work together?

This instrument (see next page) is intended to help you gauge how well your sales and marketing groups are aligned and integrated. Ask your heads of Sales and Marketing (as well as their staffs) to evaluate each of the following statements on a scale of 1 to 5, where 1 is "strongly disagree" and 5 is "strongly agree." Tally the numbers, and use the scoring key to determine the kind of relationship Sales and Marketing have in your company. The higher the score, the more integrated the relationship. (Several companies have found that their sales forces and their marketing staffs have significantly different perceptions about how well they work together—which in itself is quite interesting.)

(continued)

	Strongly Disagree 1	Disagree 2	Neither 3	Agree 4	Strongly Agree 5
1. Our sales figures are usually close to the sales forecast.					
2. If things go wrong, or results are disappointing, neither function points fingers or blames the other.					
3. Marketing people often meet with key customers during the sales process.					
4. Marketing solicits participation from Sales in drafting the marketing plan.					
5. Our salespeople believe the collateral supplied by Marketing is a valuable tool to help them get more sales.					
6. The sales force willingly cooperates in supplying feedback requested by Marketing.					
7. There is a great deal of common language here between Sales and Marketing.					
8. The heads of Sales and Marketing regularly confer about upstream issues such as idea generation, market sensing, and product development strategy.					
9. Sales and Marketing work closely together to define segment buying behavior.					
10. When Sales and Marketing meet, they do not need to spend much time on dispute resolution and crisis management.					
11. The heads of Sales and Marketing work together on business planning for products and services that will not be launched for two or more years.					

12. We discuss and use common metrics for determining the success of Sales and Marketing.					
13. Marketing actively participates in defining and executing the sales strategy for individual key accounts.					
14. Sales and Marketing manage their activities using jointly developed business funnels, processes, or pipelines that span the business chain—from initial market sensing to customer service.					
15. Marketing makes a significant contribution to analyzing data from the sales funnel and using those data to improve the predictability and effectiveness of the funnel.					
16. Sales and Marketing share a strong "We rise or fall together" culture.					
17. Sales and Marketing report to a single chief customer officer, chief revenue officer, or equivalent C-level executive.					
18. There's significant interchange of people between Sales and Marketing.					
19. Sales and Marketing jointly develop and deploy training programs, events, and learning opportunities for their respective staffs.					
20. Sales and Marketing actively participate in the preparation and presentation of each other's plans to top executives.					

___ + ___ + ___ + ___ + ___

Scoring
20-39 Undefined   60-79 Aligned
40-59 Defined   80-100 Integrated

= ___ Total

does exist, even in cases where the heads of Sales and Marketing are friendly. The sales and marketing departments in the companies we studied exhibit four types of relationships. The relationships change as the companies' marketing and sales functions mature—the groups move from being unaligned (and often conflicted) to being fully integrated (and usually conflict-free)—though we've seen only a few cases where the two functions are fully integrated.

Undefined
When the relationship is undefined, Sales and Marketing have grown independently; each is preoccupied largely with its own tasks and agendas. Each group doesn't know much about what the other is up to—until a conflict arises. Meetings between the two, which are ad hoc, are likely to be devoted to conflict resolution rather than proactive cooperation.

Defined
In a defined relationship, the two groups set up processes—and rules—to prevent disputes. There's a "good fences make good neighbors" orientation; the marketers and salespeople know who is supposed to do what, and they stick to their own tasks for the most part. The groups start to build a common language in potentially contentious areas, such as "How do we define a lead?" Meetings become more reflective; people raise questions like "What do we expect of one another?" The groups work together on large events like customer conferences and trade shows.

Aligned
When Sales and Marketing are aligned, clear boundaries between the two exist, but they're flexible. The groups engage in joint planning and training. The sales group understands and uses marketing terminology such as "value proposition" and "brand image." Marketers confer with salespeople on important accounts. They play a role in transactional, or commodity, sales as well.

Integrated
When Sales and Marketing are fully integrated, boundaries become blurred. Both groups redesign the relationship to share structures, systems, and rewards. Marketing—and to a lesser degree Sales—begins to focus on strategic, forward-thinking types of tasks (market sensing, for instance) and sometimes splits into upstream and downstream groups. Marketers are deeply embedded in the management of key accounts. The two groups develop and implement shared metrics. Budgeting becomes more flexible and less contentious. A "rise or fall together" culture develops.

We designed an assessment tool that can help organizations gauge the relationship between their sales and marketing departments. (See the exhibit "How well do Sales and Marketing work together?") We originally developed this instrument to help us understand what we were seeing in our research, but the executives we were studying quickly appropriated it for their own use. Without an objective tool of this kind, it's very difficult for managers to judge their cultures and their working environments.

Moving Up

Once an organization understands the nature of the relationship between its marketing and sales groups, senior managers may wish to create a stronger alignment between the two. (It's not always necessary, however. The exhibit "Do we need to be more aligned?" can help organizations decide whether to make a change.)

Moving from Undefined to Defined

If the business unit or company is small, members of Sales and Marketing may enjoy good, informal relationships that needn't be disturbed. This is especially true if Marketing's role is primarily to support the sales force. However, senior managers should intervene if conflicts arise regularly. As we noted earlier, this generally happens because the groups are competing for scarce resources and because their respective roles haven't been clearly defined. At this stage, managers need to create clear rules of engagement, including handoff points for important tasks like following up on sales leads.

Moving from Defined to Aligned

The defined state can be comfortable for both parties. "It may not be perfect," one VP of sales told us, "but it's a whole lot better than it was." Staying at this level won't work, though, if your industry is changing in significant ways. If the market is becoming commoditized, for example, a traditional sales force may become costly. Or if the market is moving toward customization, the sales force will need to upgrade its skills. The heads of Sales and Marketing may want to build a more aligned

Do we need to be more aligned?

The nature of relations between Sales and Marketing in your organization can run the gamut—from undefined (the groups act independent of one another) to integrated (the groups share structures, systems, and rewards). Not every company will want to—or should—move from being undefined to being defined or from being defined to being aligned. The following table can help you decide under which circumstances your company should more tightly integrate its sales and marketing functions.

	Undefined	**Defined**	**Aligned**
Don't make any changes if...	The company is small. The company has good informal relationships. Marketing is still a sales support function.	The company's products and services are fairly cut-and-dried. Traditional marketing and sales roles work in this market. There's no clear and compelling reason to change.	The company lacks a culture of shared responsibility. Sales and Marketing report separately. The sales cycle is fairly short.
Tighten the relationship between Sales and Marketing if...	Conflicts are evident between the two functions. There's duplication of effort between the functions; or tasks are falling through the cracks. The functions compete for resources or funding. → move to Defined	Even with careful definition of roles, there's duplication of effort between the functions; or tasks are falling through the cracks. The market is commoditized and makes a traditional sales force costly. Products are developed, prototyped, or extensively customized during the sales process. Product life cycles are shortening, and technology turnover is accelerating. → move to Aligned	A common process or business funnel can be created for managing and measuring revenue-generating activities. → move to Integrated

relationship and jointly add new skills. To move from a defined relationship to an aligned one, do the following.

Encourage disciplined communication. When it comes to improving relations between any two functions, the first step inevitably involves improving communication. But it's not as simple as just increasing communication between two groups. More communication is expensive. It eats up time, and it prolongs decision making. We advocate instead for more disciplined communication. Hold regular meetings between Sales and Marketing (at least quarterly, perhaps bimonthly or monthly). Make sure that major opportunities, as well as any problems, are on the agenda. Focus the discussions on action items that will resolve problems, and perhaps even create opportunities, by the next meeting. Salespeople and marketers need to know when and with whom they should communicate. Companies should develop systematic processes and guidelines such as, "You should involve the brand manager whenever the sales opportunity is above $2 million," or "We will not go to print on any marketing collateral until salespeople have reviewed it," or "Marketing will be invited to the top ten critical account reviews." Businesses also need to establish an up-to-date, user-friendly "who to call" database. People get frustrated—and they waste time—searching in the wrong places for help.

Create joint assignments; rotate jobs. As your functions become better aligned, it's important to create opportunities for marketers and salespeople to work together. This will make them more familiar with each other's ways of thinking and acting. It's useful for marketers, particularly brand managers and researchers, to occasionally go along on sales calls. They should get involved with developing alternate solutions for customers, early in the sales process. And they should also sit in on important account-planning sessions. Salespeople, in turn, should help to develop marketing plans and should sit in on product-planning reviews. They should preview ad and sales-promotion campaigns. They should share their deep knowledge about customers' purchasing habits. Jointly, marketers and salespeople should generate a playbook for expanding business with the top ten accounts in each market segment. They should also plan events and conferences together.

Appoint a liaison from Marketing to work with the sales force. The liaison needs to be someone both groups trust. He or she helps to resolve conflicts and shares with each group the tacit knowledge from the other group. It's important not to micromanage the liaison's activities. One of the Marketing respondents in our study described the liaison's role this way: "This is a person who lives with the sales force. He goes to the staff meetings, he goes to the client meetings, and he goes to the client strategy meetings. He doesn't develop product; he comes back and says, 'Here's what this market needs. Here's what's emerging,' and then he works hand in hand with the salesperson and the key customer to develop products."

Colocate marketers and salespeople. It's an old and simple truth that when people are physically close, they will interact more often and are more likely to work well together. One bank we studied located its sales and marketing functions in an empty shopping mall: Different groups and teams within Sales and Marketing were each allocated a storefront. Particularly in the early stages of moving functions toward a more closely aligned relationship, this kind of proximity is a big advantage. Most companies, though, centralize their marketing function, while the members of their sales group remain geographically dispersed. Such organizations need to work harder to facilitate communication between Sales and Marketing and to create shared work.

Improve sales force feedback. Marketers commonly complain that salespeople are too busy to share their experiences, ideas, and insights. Indeed, very few salespeople have an incentive to spend their precious time sharing customer information with Marketing. They have quotas to reach, after all, and limited time in which to meet and sell to customers. To more closely align Sales and Marketing, senior managers need to ensure that the sales force's experience can be tapped with a minimum of disruption. For instance, Marketing can ask the Sales VP to summarize any sales force insights for the month or the quarter. Or Marketing can design shorter information forms, review call reports and CRM data independently, or pay salespeople to make themselves available to interviewers from the marketing group and to summarize what their sales colleagues are thinking about.

Moving from Aligned to Integrated
Most organizations will function well when Sales and Marketing are aligned. This is especially true if the sales cycle is relatively short, the sales process is fairly straightforward, and the company doesn't have a strong culture of shared responsibility. In complicated or quickly changing situations, there are good reasons to move Sales and Marketing into an integrated relationship. (The exhibit "Sales and Marketing integration checklist" outlines the issues you'll want to think through.) This means integrating such straightforward activities as planning, target setting, customer assessment, and value-proposition development. It's tougher, though, to integrate the two groups' processes and systems; these must be replaced with common processes, metrics, and reward systems. Organizations need to develop shared databases, as well as mechanisms for continuous improvement. Hardest of all is changing the culture to support integration. The best examples of integration we found were in companies that already emphasized shared responsibility and disciplined planning; that were metrics driven; that tied rewards to results; and that were managed through systems and processes. To move from an aligned relationship to an integrated one:

Appoint a chief revenue (or customer) officer. The main rationale for integrating Sales and Marketing is that the

Sales and Marketing integration checklist

To achieve integration between Sales and Marketing, your company needs to focus on the following tasks.

Integrate activities	Integrate processes and systems	Enable the culture	Integrate organizational structures
☐ Jointly involve Sales and Marketing in product planning and in setting sales targets.	☐ Implement systems to track and manage Sales and Marketing's joint activities.	☐ Emphasize shared responsibility for results between the different divisions of the organization.	☐ Split Marketing into upstream and downstream teams.
☐ Jointly involve Sales and Marketing in generating value propositions for different market segments.	☐ Utilize and regularly update shared databases.	☐ Emphasize metrics.	☐ Hire a chief revenue officer.
☐ Jointly involve Sales and Marketing in assessing customer needs.	☐ Establish common metrics for evaluating the overall success of Sales and Marketing efforts.	☐ Tie rewards to results.	
☐ Jointly involve Sales and Marketing in signing off on advertising materials.	☐ Create reward systems to laud successful efforts by Sales and Marketing.	☐ Enforce divisions' conformity to systems and processes.	
☐ Jointly involve Sales and Marketing in analyzing the top opportunities by segment.	☐ Mandate that teams from Sales and Marketing meet periodically to review and improve relations.		
	☐ Require Sales and Marketing heads to attend each other's budget reviews with the CEO.		

two functions have a common goal: the generation of profitable and increasing revenue. It is logical to put both functions under one C-level executive. Companies such as Campbell's Soup, Coca-Cola, and FedEx have a chief revenue officer (CRO) who is responsible for planning for and delivering the revenue needed to meet corporate objectives. The CRO needs control over the forces affecting revenue—specifically, marketing, sales, service, and pricing. This manager could also be called the chief customer officer (CCO), a title used in such companies as Kellogg; Sears, Roebuck; and United Air Lines. The CCO may be more of a customer ombudsman or customer advocate in some companies; but the title can also signal an executive's broader responsibility for revenue management.

Define the steps in the marketing and sales funnels. Sales and Marketing are responsible for a sequence of activities and events (sometimes called a funnel) that leads customers toward purchases and, hopefully, ongoing relationships. Such funnels can be described from the customer's perspective or from the seller's perspective. (A typical funnel based on the customer's decision sequence is shown in the exhibit "The buying funnel.") Marketing is usually responsible for the first few steps—building customers' brand awareness and brand preference, creating a marketing plan, and generating leads for sales. Then Sales executes the marketing plan and follows up on leads. This division of labor has merit. It is simple, and it prevents Marketing from getting too involved in individual sales opportunities at the expense of

The buying funnel

There's a conventional view that Marketing should take responsibility for the first four steps of the typical buying funnel—customer awareness, brand awareness, brand consideration, and brand preference. (The funnel reflects the ways that Marketing and Sales influence customers' purchasing decisions.) Marketing builds brand preference, creates a marketing plan, and generates leads for sales before handing off execution and follow-up tasks to Sales. This division of labor keeps Marketing focused on strategic activities and prevents the group from intruding in individual sales opportunities. But if things do not go well, the blame game begins. Sales criticizes the plan for the brand, and Marketing accuses Sales of not working hard enough or smart enough.

The sales group is responsible for the last four steps of the funnel—purchase intention, purchase, customer loyalty, and customer advocacy. Sales usually develops its own funnel for the selling tasks that happen during the first two steps. (These include prospecting, defining needs, preparing and presenting proposals, negotiating contracts, and implementing the sale.) Apart from some lead generation in the prospecting stage, Marketing all too often plays no role in these tasks.

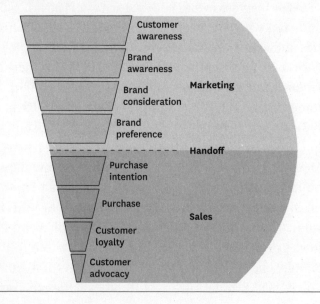

more strategic activities. But the handoff brings serious penalties. If things do not go well, Sales can say that the plan was weak, and Marketing can say that the salespeople did not work hard enough or smart enough. And in companies where Marketing makes a handoff, marketers can lose touch with active customers. Meanwhile, Sales usually develops its own funnel describing the sequence of selling tasks. Funnels of this kind—integrated into the CRM system and into sales forecasting and account-review processes—form an increasingly important backbone for sales management. Unfortunately, Marketing often plays no role in these processes. Some companies in our study, however, have integrated Marketing into the sales funnel. During prospecting and qualifying, for instance, Marketing helps Sales to create common standards for leads and opportunities. During the needs-definition stage, Marketing helps Sales develop value propositions. In the solution-development phase, Marketing provides "solution collateral"—organized templates and customizing guides so salespeople can develop solutions for customers without constantly having to reinvent the wheel. When customers are nearing a decision, Marketing contributes case study material, success stories, and site visits to help address customers' concerns. And during contract negotiations, Marketing advises the sales team on planning and pricing. Of course, Marketing's involvement in the sales funnel should be matched by Sales' involvement in the upstream, strategic decisions the marketing group is making. Salespeople should work with the marketing and R&D staffs as they decide how to segment the market, which products to offer to which segments, and how to position those products.

Split Marketing into two groups. There's a strong case for splitting Marketing into upstream (strategic) and downstream (tactical) groups. Downstream marketers develop advertising and promotion campaigns, collateral material, case histories, and sales tools. They help salespeople develop and qualify leads. The downstream team uses market research and feedback from the sales reps to help sell existing products in new market segments, to create new messages, and to design better sales tools. Upstream marketers engage in customer sensing. That is, they monitor the voice of the customer and develop a long view of the company's business opportunities and threats. The upstream team shares its insights with senior managers and product developers—and it participates in product development.

Set shared revenue targets and reward systems. The integrated organization will not succeed unless Sales and Marketing share responsibility for revenue objectives. One marketing manager told us, "I'm going to use whatever tools I need to make sure Sales is effective, because, at the end of the day, I'm judged on that sales target as well." One of the barriers to shared objectives, however, is the thorny issue of shared rewards. Salespeople historically work on commission, and marketers don't. To successfully integrate the two functions, management will need to review the overall compensation policy.

Integrate Sales and Marketing metrics. The need for common metrics becomes critical as Marketing becomes more embedded in the sales process and as Sales plays a more active role in Marketing. "In order to be the customer-intimate company we are," says Larry Norman, president of Financial Markets Group, part of the Aegon USA operating companies, "we need to be metrics driven and have metrics in place that track both sales and marketing performance." On a macro level, companies like General Electric have "the number"—the sales goal to which both Sales and Marketing commit. There is no escaping the fact that, however well integrated Sales and Marketing are, the company will also want to develop metrics to measure and reward each group appropriately.

Sales metrics are easier to define and track. Some of the most common measures are percent of sales quota achieved, number of new customers, number of sales closings, average gross profit per customer, and sales expense to total sales. When downstream marketers become embedded in the sales process—for example, as members of critical account teams—it's only logical to measure and reward their performance using sales metrics. But then how should the company evaluate its upstream marketers? On the basis of the accuracy of their product forecasting, or the number of new market segments they discover? The metrics will vary according to the type of marketing job. Senior managers need to establish different measures for brand managers, market researchers, marketing information systems managers, advertising managers, sales promotion managers, market segment managers, and product managers. It's easier to construct a set of metrics if the marketers' purposes and tasks are clearly outlined. Still, given that upstream marketers are more engaged in sowing the seeds for a better future than in helping to reap the current harvest, the metrics used to judge their performance necessarily become softer and more judgmental.

Obviously, the difference between judging current and future outcomes makes it more complicated for companies to develop common metrics for Sales and Marketing. Upstream marketers in particular need to be assessed according to what they deliver over a longer period. Salespeople, meanwhile, are in the business of converting potential demand into today's sales. As the working relationship between Sales and Marketing becomes more interactive and interdependent, the integrated organization will continue to wrestle with this difficult, but surely not insurmountable, problem.

Senior managers often describe the working relationship between Sales and Marketing as unsatisfactory. The two functions, they say, undercommunicate, underperform, and overcomplain. Not every company will want to—or should—upgrade from defined to aligned relationships or from aligned to integrated relationships. But every company can and should improve the relationship between Sales and Marketing. Carefully planned enhancements will bring salespeople's intimate knowledge of your customers into the company's core. These improvements will also help you serve customers better now and will help you build better products for the future. They will help your company marry softer, relationship-building skills with harder, analytic skills. They will force your organization to closely consider how it rewards people and whether those reward systems apply fairly across functions. Best of all, these improvements will boost both your top-line and bottom-line growth.

PHILIP KOTLER is the S.C. Johnson & Son Distinguished Professor of International Marketing at Northwestern's Kellogg School of Management. **NEIL RACKHAM** is a visiting professor at the University of Portsmouth in England. **SUJ KRISHNASWAMY** is the founder and a principal of Stinsights, a Chicago-based business strategy and market research firm.

Originally published in July 2006. Reprint R0607E

Index

Absolut, 96-97
account managers, as customer managers, 8-10
ACT brand, 105
advertising
  Aflac marketing campaigns and, 203-212
  Bic brand's meaning and, 126
  brand report card on use of, 113, 124, 127-128, 133
  Coors Brewing brand support using, 127-128
  customer value proposition and, 156
  Dell's laptop marketing campaign aimed at women and, 137-138
  Disney example of managing brand image and, 130-132
  General Electric's marketing using, 19
  Gillette's sense of product superiority using, 115
  Levi-Strauss's experience with, 111, 133-134
  long-term support for brands using, 127-128
  Michelob brand consistency and, 121
  purpose brands and, 84-85, 97-99
Aflac Cancer Center, Atlanta, 208
Aflac marketing campaigns, 203-212
  Aflac Duck creation and introduction and, 204-208
  business goals and, 208-209
  introduction of cat duck in Japan, 203-204, 209-212
all benefits type of customer value proposition, 159, 160, 161-163
Akzo Nobe (AN), 159, 172-173
alternative fuels, development of, 53, 64-66
aluminum industry, customer orientation in new products from, 45
American Express
  consumer data analysis by, 4-5
  marketing strategy of, 119-120
  Visa cards compared with cards of, 112, 119-120
American Petroleum Institute Quarterly, 73
analysis
  customer relationship management (CRM) and, 12
  market research and, 12
analytics
  customer-cultivating strategy using, 5
  customer managers and, 9
apparel industry, and female economy, 139, 142, 146-148
Apple, 100, 192
Arm & Hammer brand baking soda products, 92-93
Arnould, Eric, 194
aspirational jobs, and purpose brands, 96-97, 99
Audi brand, 193
audit (Maturity Evaluation) of marketing team, 25-27, 28-29
automotive industry
  growth cycle in, 50
  lack of attention to women's needs in, 140
  mass production and marketing approaches in, 60-63
  purpose brands and, 105-107

243

INDEX

B2B (business-to-business) companies
  customer-cultivating strategy with, 3–4
  customer managers in, 8–10
Banana Republic brand, 122, 146–147
Barzun, Jacques, 46, 76
beauty products and services industry, and female economy, 139, 142, 145–146
benefits, in customer value propositions, 159, 160, 161–163
Bentley brand, 105
Bic brand, 125–126
Black & Decker, 101
blogs, 9, 38, 138, 185, 197, 198
BMW brand, 105, 122, 193
Bolsinger, Lorraine, 31–32
Bosch, 101
Boston Consulting Group (BCG), 138, 139
Bounty paper towel brand, 140
brand audits, 113, 119, 128–129, 130
brand communities, 181–202
  business strategy with, 182, 184, 186
  community base for, 183–186
  company control vs. member control of, 183, 198–199
  consumers as focus of, 186–188
  creating a sense of contrast, conflict, and boundaries in, 185, 191–193
  design philosophy behind, 199–200
  forms of community affiliation and, 188–191
  Harley-Davidson examples of, 181, 182–186, 190, 191
  member needs and, 184
  myths about, 182–199
  online "Community Readiness Audit" on, 182
  online social networks and other online tools and, 196–198
  readiness for, 201–202
  reasons for participation in, 187
  roles of members in, 185, 193–196
  scripts used with, 199–201
  social links within, 184, 187, 190, 196–198
  using selectively as a tool in a community strategy, 195
  Vans skateboarding shoe manufacturer example of, 183, 198–199
  webs with interpersonal member links as part of, 184
brand equity
  brand report card on integrated marketing strategy to build, 111, 113, 118, 124–125
  as a bridge from past to future, 135
  consumer knowledge at heart of, 134–135
  customer equity vs., 15
  Levi-Strauss's system to measure, 111, 133–134
  managing, 109, 111
  management system for monitoring, 113, 119, 128–132, 133–134
  purpose brands and, 95
  relevancy of brand and, 112, 114–115, 117

INDEX

specific roles of different marketing activities for building, 124
value to marketers of, 135
brand equity charters, 129
brand-equity-management systems, 113, 119, 129–130, 133–134
brand managers
  brand audits used by, 128–129
  brand-building support and, 127
  brand equity charter used by, 129
  brand-equity-management systems used by, 129–130
  brand report card on understanding of different perceptions of the brand by, 113, 118–119, 125–127
  brand's meaning and, 125–127, 134
  building relationships with customers and, 2, 4
  customer managers as, 9, 10
  marketing products vs. cultivating customers and, 1–2
  specific roles of different marketing activities and, 124
brand performance
  brand report card on monitoring, 113, 119, 128–132
  customer managers and, 10
  profitability and, 1
  social concerns of women and purchase decisions and, 154
brand portfolios
  BMW's hierarchy in, 122
  brand report card hierarchy and fit in, 113, 117–118, 121–123

Gap's brands in, 122
General Motors' experience with, 122–123
brand report card, 109–135
  balancing and maximizing attributes in, 132–133
  benefits customers desire rated on, 110–114, 116
  benefits of using, 109–110, 111
  brand equity as a bridge from past to future and, 134–135
  brand portfolio hierarchy and fit rated on, 113, 117–118, 121–123
  consistency of marketing communications rated on, 112, 117, 120–121
  constructing for competitors' brands, 110, 116
  integrated marketing strategy to build equity rated on, 113, 118, 124–125
  managers' understanding of perceptions of the brand rated on, 113, 118–119, 125–127
  monitoring brand performance using, 133–134
  positioning of brand rated on, 112, 117, 118–120
  price based on perceptions of brand value rated on, 112, 115–117
  relevancy of brand on, 112, 114–115, 117
  sources of brand equity monitored on, 113, 119, 128–132
  summary of ten attributes of, 110, 112–113
  sustained support for brand awareness rated on, 113, 119, 127–128

INDEX

brand report card (*continued*)
  understanding a brand's meaning using, 125–127, 134
  using to rate a brand, 116–119
brands
  advertising for building, 98–99
  audits of, 113, 119, 128–129, 130
  brand-equity-measurement system for clarifying meaning of, 134
  brand report card for understanding meaning of, 134
  broken paradigm of market segmentation and, 82–86
  consumers' perceptions of value of, 112, 115–117
  Disney example of managing, 113, 130–132
  failure of new brands and need for new marketing model in, 81–82, 83, 107
  understanding of perceptions of, 113, 118–119, 125–127
  understanding the meaning of, 125–127, 134
Braun brand, 127
budgets
  conflicts between Sales and Marketing over, 221–222
  customer managers and, 8
buggy whip industry, 58, 64
Buick brand, 123
Burning Man, 194
business schools, and focus on cultivating customers, 9
buying funnel, in Sales and Marketing alignment, 235–237

Cadillac brand, 123
Calvin Klein brand, 119
Campaign for Real Beauty, Dove brand, 185, 192
Campbell's Soup, 235
Cascade automatic-dishwashing detergent brand, 115–116
Cayenne SUV brand, Porsche, 192–193
Cellular Cream Platinum Rare antiaging moisturizer, 146
Center of Excellence (COE), GE, 36–37
chemicals industry, growth in, 49
Chevrolet brand, 123
chief customer officers (CCOs)
  description of, 7–8
  R&D and, 13
  reimagining the marketing department with, 3, 11
  Sales and Marketing alignment and, 233–325
chief revenue officers (CROs), in Sales and Marketing alignment, 233–325
Chopra, Deepak, 191
Chrysler, 7
Church & Dwight, 92–93
Citigroup, 220
clothing industry, and female economy, 139, 142, 146–148
clubs, as part of brand communities, 186, 194, 201
CLV. *See* customer lifetime value
chief marketing officers (CMOs)
  chief customer officers (CCOs) vs., 3, 7, 11
  marketing at GE with, 24–25, 28, 31, 35
Coca-Cola, 113, 124–125, 192, 198, 220, 235

INDEX

Colgate-Palmolive, 93
colocation of staff, in Sales and Marketing alignment, 232
commercial innovation, at GE, 23
communication
   building relationships with customers and, 2, 4
   direct, between customers and firms, 2
   marketing products vs. cultivating customers in, 2–3
   Sales and Marketing alignment and, 230
communities, as base for brand communities, 183–186
community affiliation, and brand communities, 188–191
competition
   brand communities and, 184
   brand report card on positioning of brand and, 112, 117, 118–120
   brand report cards for brands of, 110, 116
   growth industries and, 47–48, 49, 54–55
conflict, in brand communities, 185, 191–193
consistency of marketing communications
   brand report card on, 112, 117, 120–121
   Michelob brand advertising and, 121
control of brand communities, 183, 198–199
Cooper, Lee, 34, 35
Coors Brewing Company, 127–128
Coors Light brand, 127–128

Corning Glass Works, 44
cosmetics industry, and female economy, 145–146
Cossery, Jean-Michel, 29–30
Courtyard by Marriott, 85, 101, 104
credit cards
   marketing strategy of, 112, 119–120
   women consumers and, 149, 150
Crest brand, 96, 102–103, 104–105
CRM. *See* customer relationship management
Curves fitness chain, 139, 144–145
customer data collection
   American Express's use of, 5–6
   chief customer officers (CCOs) and, 7–8, 11
   customer managers and, 9
   customer relationship management (CRM) and, 11–12
   customer service interactions and, 13–14
   levels of information tracked in, 16–17
   marketing research for, 2
   sales statistics and, 2
   Tesco's use of, 5
customer departments
   customer-facing functions in, 10
   customer relationship management (CRM) in, 10–12
   customer service and, 13–14
   market research in, 12
   reinventing marketing departments as, 3, 7, 11
   research and development in, 12–13

INDEX

customer equity
  brand equity vs., 15
  chief customer officers (CCOs) and, 8
  market research and, 12
  marketing activities tracked for, 17
  metrics for, 15–16
customer equity share, 15, 16
customer experience, brand report card on, 110–114, 116
customer lifetime value (CLV)
  chief customer officers (CCOs) and, 8
  current sales statistics vs., 14–15
  customer managers and, 10
  customer profitability focus and, 14
  data sources for, 16
  market research and, 12
  need for, 14–15
customer managers
  description of work of, 9
  marketing rethinking using, 8–10
  product managers vs., in building relationships, 1, 3, 4, 10
  training of, 9
customer metrics
  audit (Maturity Evaluation) at GE and, 25–27, 28–29
  chief customer officers (CCOs) and, 8
  current sales statistics vs., 14–15
  customer-cultivating strategies and, 3, 4, 14–17
  customer equity focus of, 15–16
  customer equity share and, 16
  customer managers and, 10
  customer profitability focus of, 14
  financial statements and reporting of, 15
  levels of information tracked in, 16–17
  managers' use of, 17
  Sales and Marketing alignment with, 239–240
  shift in approach to, 15
customer needs
  brand communities and, 184
  brand report card on meeting, 110–114, 116
  customer-cultivating strategy with focus on, 3–4
  customer managers and, 8–10
  customer relationship management (CRM) and, 11
  faith in mass production in automobile industry vs., 60–62
  growth by meeting, 43
  market segments related to, 82
customer orientation
  brand communities and, 186–188
  brand report card on meeting, 110–114, 116
  product orientation with, 44–45
  railroads' product orientation vs., 41–42
  research orientation vs., 44, 45, 51, 58, 60–61, 66, 69–71, 75
  rethinking marketing and cultivating, 2–6
  successful new products from, 45

customer profitability, focus on, 14, 15
customer relationship management (CRM)
    customer department's responsibility for, 11–12
    IT groups and, 10–11
    marketing products vs. cultivating customers and, 2–3
    sales force feedback using, 232
customer relationships
    building, 2, 4
    chief customer officers (CCOs) and, 7–8, 11
    customer managers and, 8–10
    customer service and, 13–14
    direct communication in, 2
    marketing products vs. cultivating customers in, 2–3, 4
    reimagining the marketing department and, 11
customers
    building relationships with, 2, 4
    chief customer officers (CCOs) and, 7–8
    cultivating, as part of rethinking marketing, 2–6
    customer manager's interaction with, 9
    customer-cultivating strategy with focus on needs of, 3–4
    data collection on, 2
    direct communication between firms and, 2–3
    expectations of, 1–2
    leaders and focus on satisfying, 77–79
    marketing products vs. cultivating, 2–3, 4
    research and development with input from, 12–13
customer service
    customer department with, 3, 13–14
    Delta's experience with, 13–14
    outsourcing, 14
customer value propositions, 155–179
    advertising and promotional use of, 156–157
    all benefits type of, 159, 160, 161–163
    building blocks of, 162
    business strategy and performance and, 175–179
    as a central business skill, 159
    demonstrating customer value in advance in, 172–173
    documenting value delivered in, 159, 173–175
    favorable points of difference type of, 159, 160, 163–164
    kinds of, 159, 160
    points of contention in, 162
    points of difference in, 162
    points of parity in, 162
    resin company example of use of, 157, 168–169
    resonating focus type of, 159, 160, 164–170, 177–178
    substantiating value claims in, 158–159, 170–172
    understanding customers' businesses and, 158
    value calculators in, 172
    value case histories in, 172
    value generation planning (VGP) process and tools in, 174
    value word equations and, 171

INDEX

data collection
   American Express's use of, 5–6
   chief customer officers (CCOs) and, 7–8, 11
   customer managers and, 9
   customer relationship management (CRM) and, 11–12
   customer service interactions and, 13–14
   levels of information tracked in, 16–17
   marketing research for, 2
   sales statistics and, 2
   Tesco's use of, 5
declining unit costs, and growth industry cycles, 50, 59, 64–67
Dell, 137–138, 192
DeLoach, Harris, Jr., 176
Delta Airlines, customer service at, 13–14
Disney brand, 98, 113, 130–132
disruptive innovations, and purpose brands, 91, 94–95, 102
distribution channels
   customer-cultivating strategies and, 3
   market research and, 12
Dove brand, Campaign for Real Beauty, 185, 192
dry cleaning industry, growth in, 46–47
Dudzinski, Mark, 36, 37
DuPont, 43, 44, 52

EasyShare digital cameras, 95
eBay, 90, 96, 98
Ecomagination, GE, 24
Edison, Thomas, 55

electric utilities industry, growth in, 47–48
electronics industry
   dependence on technical research and development in, 69–72, 75
   growth cycle in, 49, 50
   emotional dimensions of customer jobs, and purpose brands, 87–90
endorser brands, 100–101, 102, 104, 105
Estée Lauder, 13
"everyday low pricing" (EDLP) strategy, Procter & Gamble, 112, 116–117
executives
   brand communities and involvement of, 185–186
   chief customer officers (CCOs) and, 7–8
   lack of growth and failure of, 41–42
Express stores, 147

Facebook, 187
facial skin-care products, and women consumers, 145–146
favorable points of difference type of customer value proposition, 159, 160, 163–164
feature fatigue, 12
Federal Express (FedEx), 83, 94–96, 235
feedback, to sales force, 232–233
female economy, 137–154. *See also* women
   apparel industry and, 146–148

250

beauty products and services industry and, 145-146
businesses owned by women in, 152-153
consumer spending controlled by, 137, 147
Dell's laptop marketing campaign and, 137-138
financial services industry and, 148-149, 150
fitness industry and, 144-145
food industry and, 142-144
as growth market, 137, 139, 140, 154
health care industry and, 149-151
increase in number of working women and, 140-141
industries with greatest opportunities for, 139, 141-142
lack of products and services designed specifically for, 139-140
number of working women and, 140-141, 162-153
six key consumer segments in, 141, 142-143
social concerns of women and purchase decisions in, 154
time issues and purchases in, 151-152, 153
film industry, lack of customer orientation in, 42-43, 58
financial planning software, 86
financial services companies
customer-cultivating strategies of, 6
customer managers in, 10
women consumers and, 139, 142, 148-149, 150

financial statements, customer-centered metrics reported on, 15
Firefox, 13
fishfulthinking.com, 188
fitness industry, and female economy, 139, 142, 144-145
501 brand of jeans, 133-134
food industry, and female economy, 139, 142-144
Foote, Cone & Belding, 134
Ford, Henry, 62-63
Ford Motor Company, 98
functional dimensions of customer jobs, and purpose brands, 87-90

Galbraith, John Kenneth, 59
Gap Inc., 113, 122, 147
Garnier brand, 197
GE Aviation, 19-20, 28, 31-33
GE Capital, Americas, 34-35
GE Energy, 36-37
GE Healthcare, 24, 28, 29-31
GE Infrastructures Water & Process Technologies (GEIW&PT), 172, 174, 175-176
General Electric (GE)
audit (Maturity Evaluation) of marketing team at, 25-27, 28-29
Center of Excellence (COE) at, 36-37
commercial innovation at, 23
cross-company initiatives at 23-24
Ecomagination at, 24
growth strategy of, 20-21
Imagination Breakthroughs at, 24

INDEX

General Electric (GE) (*continued*)
  implementer role at, 27, 35-37
  innovator role at, 27, 31-33
  instigator role at, 27-31
  integrator role at, 27, 33-35
  marketer's DNA (roles) at, 27, 37-38
  marketing approach of, 19-39
  marketing engine framework for, 21, 22, 26-27
  marketing leadership at, 24-37
  marketing function at, 19-22, 23-24, 220
  MarkNet social network at, 38
  need for new marketing engine at, 20-21
  people (marketers) at, 21, 22, 26, 27
  principles (common language and standards) at, 21, 22, 26-27
  process (metrics for sales and marketing performance) at, 21, 22, 27, 239
General Mills, 220
General Motors, 52, 122-123
Gentile, Thomas, 20, 33
Gillette brand, 113
  relevancy of, 112, 114-115
  protection of, by Gillette, 126-127
Gleem brand, 102
Goldblatt, Barry, 92
Goldfish brand, 188
Gold's Gym, 184, 187
Google, 90, 98
Greeter role, in brand communities, 185, 195
grocery stores
  cycle of growth and obsolescence in, 48-49, 58
  women consumers and, 143-144
growth
  customer-oriented management and, 43-44
  DuPont's strategy for, 43
  GE's strategy for, 20-21
  management failure and lack of, 41-42
growth industries
  belief in lack of a competitive substitute for its major product in, 46, 50, 54-58
  cycle of expansion and obsolescence in, 50-51
  declining unit costs lack of innovation in, 50, 59, 64-67
  dependence on technical research and development and, 69-72, 75
  examples of, 46-49
  expanding population and profitability myth about, 50, 51-53
  mass production and marketing approaches in, 50, 59-63
growth market, women customers as, 137
Gucci brand, 96-97

H&M, 147-148
Hannah Montana brand, 191
Hansen, Morten, 9
Harley-Davidson brand, 98, 119
  brand community built by, 181, 182-186, 190, 191
  scripts used by, 200-201
Harley-Davidson Museum, 184, 190, 201

Harley Owners Group (H.O.G.) membership club, 186, 201
Harte-Hanks survey, 10–11
Hasbro, 198
health clubs, and women consumers, 139, 144–145
health care industry, and female economy, 139, 142, 149–151
Henson, Dan, 34
Hershey's, 7
Hole Hawg brand, 101, 102, 104
Honda brand, 123
hub affiliation, and brand communities, 188, 189, 191

IBM
  customer managers at, 9
  Insurance Process Acceleration Framework of, 3–4
  marketing function at, 220
Imagination Breakthroughs, at GE, 24
Immelt, Jeff, 21, 23
implementer marketer role, GE, 27, 35–37
innovation
  brand-equity-measurement system for monitoring, 134
  customer focus of, 13
  innovator marketer role at GE and, 27, 31–33
  marketing at General Electric and, 20, 21, 23
  petroleum industry and, 53, 55–56, 65–67
innovator marketer role, GE, 27, 31–33
instigator marketer role, GE, 27–31

insurance companies
  customer-cultivating strategies of, 6
  women consumers and, 149, 150
Insurance Process Acceleration Framework, IBM, 3–4
integrator marketer role, GE, 27, 33–35
Intel, 31
Intergraph, 166–167, 171
International Flavors and Fragrances, 13
investment services, and women consumers, 149, 150
iPod brand, 100
IT groups, and customer relationship management (CRM), 10–11
IT resources, and customer service interactions, 14

Japan, Aflac marketing campaigns in, 203–204, 209–212
jeans brands, 133–134
job rotation, in Sales and Marketing alignment, 230–231
Johnson & Johnson, 151
Jordan, Michael, 191
Jump Associates, 199

Kaiser Aluminum & Chemical Corporation, 45
Kaplan Thaler Group, 205–206
Kellogg, 235
kerosene industry, 47, 52, 54, 55
Kiehl's brand, 197
Kirchart, Heath, 191
Kodak, 94–95, 96
Kraft, 220

Lafley, A.G., 81, 107
Lamborghini brand, 193
LAN Airlines, 33
La Prairie, 146
La Roche-Posay brand, 197
leadership, satisfying customers as focus of, 77–79
Lever Brothers, 115–116
Levi-Strauss, 111, 133–134
Levitt, Theodore, 82, 85
liaison, in Sales and Marketing alignment, 231
Limited Brands, 147
L'Oréal, 185, 197–198
loss leaders, 14

Macy's, 98
Makita, 101
management
  growth and customer orientation of, 43–44
  growth cycle of expansion and obsolescence and, 51
  lack of growth and failure of, 41–42
managers
  brand report card on understanding of consumers' different perceptions of the brand by, 113, 118–119, 125–127
  metrics used by, 17
marketing
  brand equity and, 135
  failure of new brands and need for new model in, 81–82, 83, 107
  selling vs., 59–60
  understanding the consumer vs. understanding the job in, 90–91

marketing department
  market research used by, 12
  reinventing as a customer department, 7, 11
  research and development integrated with, 12–13
  sales department and. *See* Sales and Marketing alignment
  upstream and downstream groups in, 238
marketing myopia, 41–79
  belief in lack of a competitive substitute for major product in, 54–58
  cycle of expansion and obsolescence in, 50–51
  dependence on technical research and development in, 69–72, 75
  expanding population and profitability myth in, 50, 51–53
  faith in mass production and marketing approaches in, 60–63
marketing program
  Aflac's campaign in Japan, 203–212
  brand communities as part of, 182, 184, 186
  brand report card for guiding, 134
  Coca-Cola's example of range of activities in, 124–125
  consistency of communications rated in, 112, 117, 120–121
  integrated strategy to build equity rated in, 113, 118, 124–125

sustained support for brand
awareness rated in, 113,
119, 127-128
tracking for metrics, 16-17
marketing, rethinking, 1-17
building relationships with
customers and, 2, 4
change of strategy and structure needed for, 2
chief customer officers (CCOs)
and, 7-8
cultivating customers as part
of, 2-6
customer-facing functions
and, 10-13
customer managers and, 8-10
customer metrics and, 14-17
customer relationship management (CRM) and, 10-12
customer service and, 13-14
marketing department reinvented as the customer
department in, 7
market research and, 12
older approach of marketing
products and need for,
1-2, 3
reinventing marketing as part
of, 6-14
research and development
and, 12-13
marketing team, GE
audit (Maturity Evaluation) of,
25-27, 28-29
implementer role on, 27, 35-37
innovator role on, 27, 31-33
instigator role on, 27-31
integrator role on, 27, 33-35
market research
customer data collection in, 2
customer department's responsibility for, 12

market segmentation
brand portfolio hierarchy and
fit rated for, 113, 117-118,
121-123
broken paradigm of, 82-86
customer needs ignored in, 82
data collection on, 16
failure of new brands and
need for new model of,
81-82, 83
in female economy, 141,
142-143
how customers have jobs and
hire products to do them
reflected in, 82, 85-86
social, functional, and emotional dimensions of customer jobs and, 87-90
type of customers as basis for,
82-84
understanding the consumer
vs. understanding the job
in, 90-91
market share, vs. customer equity share, 15, 16
MarkNet social network, GE, 38
Marriott International, 85, 101,
104
mass media communications, 1,
2, 3, 4, 17
mass production
cycles in growth industries
and, 50, 59-63
selling vs. marketing in,
59-60
Maturity Evaluation (audit) of
GE marketing team,
25-27, 28-29
membership clubs, as part of
brand communities, 186,
194, 201
Menon, Anil, 214

INDEX

Mentor role, in brand communities, 185, 195
Mercedes-Benz brand, 105, 118–119
metrics
  audit (Maturity Evaluation) at GE and, 25–27, 28–29
  chief customer officers (CCOs) and, 8
  current sales statistics vs., 14–15
  customer-cultivating strategies and, 3, 4, 14–17
  customer equity focus of, 15–16
  customer equity share and, 16
  customer managers and, 10
  customer profitability focus of, 14
  financial statements and reporting of, 15
  levels of information tracked in, 16–17
  managers' use of, 17
  Sales and Marketing alignment with, 239–240
  shift in approach to, 15
MGB car clubs, 194
Michelob, 112, 121
Microsoft, 192, 198, 220
Milwaukee Electric Tool, 101–102, 104
Modine, Austin, 138
Montblanc brand, 97
Morita, Akio, 91–92
movie industry, lack of customer orientation in, 42–43, 58
Mozilla, 13
myEngines, GE Aviation, 32–33

National Wholesale Grocers, 48
natural gas industry, 56–57

needs of customers
  brand communities and, 184
  brand report card on meeting, 110–114, 116
  customer-cultivating strategy with focus on, 3–4
  customer managers and, 8–10
  customer relationship management (CRM) and, 11
  faith in mass production in automobile industry vs., 60–62
  growth by meeting, 43
  market segments related to, 82
New Jersey Retail Grocers Association, 48
New York Times, 138
Nijdra Groep, 172
Nike, 191
Nike+ online community, 191
Nissan, 98
Nokia, 12–13
Nokia Beta Labs, 13
Nordstrom, 119
Norman, Larry, 239

oil industry. *See* petroleum industry
Olay brand, 146
Old Navy brand, 113, 122
Oldsmobile brand, 123
Olympics, 125
Omidyar, Pierre, 90
online communities, and brand communities, 187, 188, 191
opinion leaders, and brand communities, 193
Oracle, 7
Oral B brand, 127

organizational structure, and brand communities, 186
Outdoorseiten brand, 187
outsourcing, of customer service, 14

Pelino, Dan, 214
Pepperidge Farm, 187–188
Pepsi, 192
Pepsi Challenge, 192
perceptions of a brand
   managers' understanding of, 113, 118–119, 125–127
   price based on, 112, 115–117
petrochemical industry, growth of, 57–58
petroleum industry
   belief in lack of a competitive substitute for major product in, 54–58
   customer needs and fuel sources supported by, 67–69
   customers and marketing in, 72–76
   expanding population and profitability myth in, 50, 51–53
   focus on efficiency of getting and making its product, 53–54
   growth cycle in, 50–51
   innovations from outside the industry, 53, 55–56, 65–67
points of contention, in customer value propositions, 162
points of difference, in customer value propositions, 162
points of parity, in customer value propositions, 162

Pontiac brand, 123
pool affiliation, and brand communities, 188–190, 191
population growth, and profitability in growth industries, 50, 51–53
Porsche brand, 105, 192–193
positioning of brand
   brand report card on, 112, 117, 118–120
   Visa credit cards' marketing strategy for, 112, 119–120
Pour Your Heart Into It (Schultz and Yang), 111
Pratt & Whitney, 20
pricing
   brand-equity-measurement system for monitoring consumers' reactions to, 134
   brand report card on consumers' perceptions of brand value and, 112, 115–117, 132–133
   of clothing, and women consumers, 147–148
   "everyday low pricing" (EDLP) strategy of Procter & Gamble, 112, 116–117
Procter & Gamble (P&G)
   account managers for major retailers at, 8–10
   Church & Dwight's growth compared with, 93
   collaboration of users and producers at, 13
   Crest purpose brand of, 96, 102–103, 104–105
   customer managers at, 9
   "everyday low pricing" (EDLP) strategy of, 112, 116–117

Procter & Gamble (*continued*)
   innovation at, 33
   marketing function at, 220
   model for marketing and, 81
   Olay brand of, 146
   Swiffer product introduction by, 90
   value-pricing strategy of, 112, 115–116
product development
   aluminum industry example of customer uses in, 45
   customer input needed in, 12–13
   customer orientation vs. product or research orientation in, 45
   dependence on technical research and, 50, 69–72, 75
   how customers have jobs and hire products to do them reflected in, 82, 85–86
   instigator role at GE Healthcare and, 29–31
   social, functional, and emotional dimensions of customer jobs and, 87–90
   understanding the consumer vs. understanding the job in, 90–91
product managers
   customer managers vs., in building relationships, 1, 3, 4, 10
   reimagining marketing departments and, 11
product obsolescence
   cycle of expansion and, 50–51, 58
   petroleum industry example of belief in lack of a competitive substitute and, 54–58
product orientation
   automobile industry and, 61–62
   customer orientation vs., in rethinking marketing 2–6
   customer orientation needed with, 44–45
   failure of railroad business and, 41–42, 43
   film industry and, 42–43
   textile companies in New England and, 44–45
profitability
   brand performance and, 1
   customer managers and, 10
   low unit production costs and, 64
   population growth and, in growth industries, 50, 51–53
   focus on customer vs. product, 14, 15
   mass production in automobile industry and, 62–63
purchase patterns, customer-cultivating strategies based on, 5, 6
purpose brands, 81–107
   advertising's role of linking jobs to, 84–85, 97–99
   broken paradigm of market segmentation and, 82–86
   Church & Dwight's baking soda business example of, 92–93
   definition of, 93–94
   developing different products addressing a common job and, 85, 91–92

disruptive innovations and, 91, 94–95, 102
endorser brands vs., 100–101
extending, 85, 99–105
failure of new brands and need for new marketing model in, 81–82, 83, 107
FedEx example of, 83, 94–96
feelings and aspirational jobs with, 96–97, 99
identifying new, related jobs for, 85, 92–94
improving the product by understanding the job in, 90–91
Marriott's example of, 101
Milwaukee Electric Tool's examples of, 101–102
observing consumers in action and, 84, 91–92
P&G's Crest brand example of, 102–103, 104–105
social, functional, and emotional dimensions of customer jobs and, 87–90
Sony's Walkman brand example of, 85, 91–92, 100, 104

Quaker Chemical, 159, 175, 177–178
Quicken Financial Planner, 86
QuietCare home sensing system, 30–31

railroads
lack of customer orientation in, 41–42, 43
cycle of growth and obsolescence in, 58
transportation as focus of, 45–46, 76–77
R&D. *See* research and development
Range Rover brand, 105
Red Hat Society, 194
Register, The, 138
Reivich, Karen, 188
relationships with customers
building, 2, 4
chief customer officers (CCOs) and, 7–8, 11
customer managers and, 8–10
customer service and, 13–14
direct communication in, 2
marketing products vs. cultivating customers in, 2–3, 4
reimagining the marketing department and, 11
relevancy of a brand
brand-equity-measurement system for monitoring, 134
brand report card on, 112, 114–115, 117
report card. *See* brand report card
research and development (R&D)
customer department's responsibility for, 3, 12–13
growth industries and dependence on, 69–72, 75
innovation at GE and, 31, 34
marketing integrated with, 12–13
petroleum industry and alternative fuel sources and, 64–66
support for a brand using, 119
research orientation, customer orientation vs., 44, 45, 51, 58, 60–61, 66, 69–71, 75

Residence Inn by Marriott, 101, 104
resonating focus type of customer value proposition, 159, 160, 164–170
   crafting, 168–169, 170
   examples of, 165–170
   favorable points of difference type vs., 164–165
   training program for, 177–178
reward systems, in Sales and Marketing alignment, 238
Reynolds Metals Company, 45
Rockefeller, John D., 52
Rockwell Automation, 158, 171–172
roles, in brand communities, 185
Rolls-Royce brand, 20, 105
Rosenbaum, Mark, 197

Saddleback Church, Orange County, California, 185, 194–195
Sales and Marketing alignment, 213–241
   competition and integration of teams in, 215
   creating a stronger alignment in, 228–240
   determining their existing relationship in, 216
   instrument for gauging relationships between, 223–225
   marketing function variations from company to company, 218–220
   determining need for, 229
   result of lack of alignment, 213–214
   situations for creating more interconnection in, 216–217
   sources of friction between Sales and Marketing and, 220–223
   study to identify best practices for, 213–218
   types of relationships in, 223–227
sales statistics
   customer lifetime value (CLV) vs., 14–15
   data collection on customers using, 2
sales support
   at General Electric, 19, 22–23, 33–34
   mass production and, 59–60
Samsung, 7
Saturn brand, 119, 123
Sawzall brand, 101, 102, 104
Schau, Hope, 194
Schultz, Howard, 110–111
Scoble, Robert, 198
scripts, brand communities, 199–201
Sears, Roebuck, 7, 235
segment managers
   customer managers and, 10, 11
   customer service and, 13–14
segments
   brand portfolio hierarchy and fit rated for, 113, 117–118, 121–123
   broken paradigm of, 82–86
   customer needs ignored in, 82
   data collection on, 16
   failure of new brands and need for new model of, 81–82, 83

in female economy, 141,
    142–143
how customers have jobs and
    hire products to do them
    reflected in, 82, 85–86
social, functional, and emo-
    tional dimensions of
    customer jobs and,
    87–90
type of customers as basis for,
    82–84
understanding the consumer
    vs. understanding the job
    in, 90–91
selling, marketing vs., 59–60
shareholder value, and customer
    equity, 16
Shell Oil Company, 127
Sloan, Alfred P., 122–123
social concerns of women, and
    purchase decisions, 154
social dimensions of customer
    jobs, and purpose brands,
    87–90
social links, in brand communi-
    ties, 184, 187, 190
social networks, and brand com-
    munities, 196–198
Société Bic, 125
Sonoco, 165–166, 176–177
Sony, 85, 91–92, 100, 104,
    118–119
Spohrer, Jim, 9
Starbucks, 96, 110–114, 184, 187,
    192
Storyteller role, in brand com-
    munities, 185, 195
strategy
    brand communities as part of,
        182, 184, 186
    customer value propositions
        as part of, 175–176, 178

marketing at General Electric
    and, 19, 21
Sun Microsystems, 7
supermarkets
    cycle of growth and obsoles-
        cence in, 48–49, 58
    women consumers and,
        143–144
Swiffer home cleaning product
    brand, 13, 90
Swords, Tim, 32–33

technical research and develop-
    ment, dependence on, 50,
    69–72, 75
Tesco
    loyalty card data and analytics
        at, 5
    manager interaction with cus-
        tomers in, 7–8
    women's preference for,
        143–144
Tesco Week in Store (TWIST)
    program, 8
textile companies, product ori-
    entation of, 44–45
Tide brand, 131
Toyota brand, 105, 123
Trekkies, 194

Unilever, 84–85, 93, 97–98
United Airlines, 7, 235
UPS, 95
USAA, 7
usage imagery, 114, 119
user imagery, 114, 119, 123

value calculators, 172
value case histories, 172

value generation planning (VGP) process and tools, 174
value word equations, 171
Vans skateboarding shoe manufacturer, 183, 198–199
Virgin brand, 97
Visa credit cards, marketing strategy of, 112, 119–120
Volvo brand, 105

Wachovia, 7
Walkman brand, 85, 91–92, 100, 104
Wall Street Journal, 5
Warped Tour, 199
web affiliation, and brand communities, 188, 189, 190
Web online communities, 187, 188, 191, 196–198
Whole Foods, 143
women, 137–154. *See also* female economy
   apparel industry and, 146–148
   beauty products and services industry and, 145–146
   businesses owned by, 152–153
   consumer spending controlled by, 137, 147
   Dell's laptop marketing campaign aimed at, 137–138
   financial services industry and, 148–149, 150
   fitness industry and, 144–145
   food industry and, 142–144
   as growth market, 137, 139, 140, 154
   health care industry and, 149–151
   increase in number of working women, 140–141
   industries with greatest opportunities for sales to, 139, 141–142
   lack of products and services designed specifically for, 139–140
   number of working women, 140–141, 162–153
   six key consumer segments in, 141, 142–143
   social concerns of, and purchase decisions, 154
   surveys and interviews of, 138–140
   time issues and purchases by, 151–152, 153
Woods, Tiger, 191
World of Coca-Cola museum, Atlanta, 125

Yang, Dori Jones, 111

Zima brand, 127

You don't want to miss these...

We've combed through hundreds of *Harvard Business Review* articles on key management topics and selected *the* most important ones to help you maximize your own and your organization's performance.

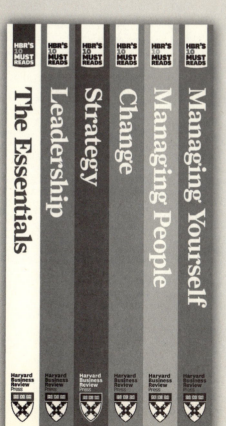

10 Must-Read Articles on:

LEADERSHIP
How can you transform yourself from a good manager into an extraordinary leader?

STRATEGY
Is your company spending an enormous amount of time and energy on strategy development, with little to show for its efforts?

MANAGING YOURSELF
The path to your own professional success starts with a critical look in the mirror.

CHANGE
70 percent of all change initiatives fail. Learn how to turn the odds in your company's favor.

MANAGING PEOPLE
What really motivates people? How do you deal with problem employees? How can you build a team that is greater than the sum of its parts?

THE ESSENTIALS
If you read nothing else, read these 10 articles from some of *Harvard Business Review*'s most influential authors.

Yours for only $24.95 each.
10 articles in each collection.
Available in PDF or paperback.

Order online at mustreads.hbr.org
or call us at 800-668-6780.
Outside the U.S. and Canada,
call +1 617-783-7450.